College Countdown

The Parent's and Student's Survival Kit for the College Admissions Process

Jill F. VonGruben, M.A.

McGraw-Hill

New York • San Francisco • Washington, D.C. • Auckland • Bogotá
Caracas • Lisbon • London • Madrid • Mexico City • Milan
Montreal • New Delhi • San Juan • Singapore
Sydney • Tokyo • Toronto

Library of Congress Catalog Card Number: 99-75850

McGraw-Hill

A Division of The McGraw-Hill Companies

1 2 3 4 5 6 7 8 9 0 AGM/AGM 9 0 9 8 7 6 5 4 3 2 1 0 9

ISBN 0-07-135290-2

This book was set in Sabon and Franklin Gothic Condensed by TopDesk Publishers' Group. Printed and bound by Quebecor Martinsburg.

This book is printed on recycled, acid-free paper containing a minimum of 50% recycled, de-inked fiber.

Contents

Introduction *vii*

Praise for Taming the Paper Monster *xiii*

Acknowledgments *xvii*

Chapter 1: On Your Mark—The Survival Skills—Having What It Takes 1

Chapter 2: Get Set—The College Game Starts in 8th Grade 17

Chapter 3: Go!—9th Grade—The Clock Starts 43

Chapter 4: 10th Grade—The Clock is Ticking 67

Chapter 5: If Only Money Did Grow On Trees—Paying for College 87

Chapter 6: 11th Grade—The Halfway Mark 119

Chapter 7: The Final Countdown 165

Chapter 8: Planning Ahead When You Have Special Concerns 197

Chapter 9: Those Last Few Minutes 209

Appendix: College Call Checklist 221

Glossary 231

References 235

Index 247

Introduction

The checklists (which are included) were the beginning of this book's precursor, *Taming the Paper Monster: The College Game (And It Starts in 8th Grade!).*

The checklists were the result of the journey our family took in getting our oldest through the college application process. We learned much during these journeys. We made our fair share of mistakes along the way. For these reasons, we decided to share the lists with other high school families in our school district.

The basic form of the College Countdown timeline came from discussions with these other families. We were all stumbling along in our own journeys, hitting some steps while missing others. As the checklists and countdown spread from family-to-family, parents and educators suggested to me to pull it together into a book. The reason was so that no other family would stumble along in the dark, which makes the journey so much longer and stressful than it is already.

The resulting book attempted to pull together all those pieces of paper a family accumulates into one place to help make it easier to get all the steps done in the proper order. As more families and teachers gave me additional hints and tricks, I'd add them to the next version of the book. *Taming the Paper Monster* evolved into the current *THE COLLEGE COUNTDOWN: A Parent's and Student's Survival Kit for the College Admissions Process*. A note to the evolutionary process is recognition to Tracy L. VonGruben who provided the artwork in Taming the Paper Monster.

As you discover the hints and tricks of the trade, share them with your friends and high school guidance counselor. Share the wealth. It pays dividends! As you discover your own individual hints and tricks (and you will), please share them with me so that I may share them with other families in a future edition of THE COLLEGE COUNTDOWN. You can e-mail them to me at wldcoprs@aol.com. I hope you enjoy this book as much as I have enjoyed putting it together.

Rules of the game

The college application game is not for the faint of heart. If the following checklists and advice appear on the surface to be mind-boggling, exciting, time consuming, a full-time job, frightening, exhilarating and completely insane; you're only partially correct. It's more! This journey will have times of tears and hopefully times of great laughter and fun.

It takes a total family commitment in partnership with your high school advisors, support personnel, and school district administration to allow this game to end with you studying in the best possible university choice. To paraphrase an AT&T commercial aired during the '96 Olympics - "Imagine a world without limits - where anything is possible. When people communicate, there is no limit to what people can do!" It will take all the help you can acquire.

The college application game, in truth, starts the first day you entered school in Kindergarten. Each experience, each risk taken builds on the previous to mold and enrich you.

The actual game-clock doesn't start running when you are a high school junior. It starts in the 8th Grade (or earlier) when you (and hopefully your parents) sit down and plan your four academic years of high school.

Teens, it is your job to hold up your part of the bargain also. You need to pay attention in classes, do the assigned readings and projects, and participate fully in classroom discussions. This is your ownership in your course work and your high school diploma. No one is just going to, or should, just hand it to you. It takes hard work and a lot of fun along the way.

Businesses and graduate programs are looking for college graduates who are not just trained in a specific curriculum, but who also have advanced skills and a variety of experiences. Skills are, but not limited to, the following categories: quantitative, communication, leadership, persuasive and technical/scientific. Colleges are looking for high school graduates with these same attributes. Colleges and universities are looking for total-package kids. The areas they are looking for are, but not limited to, academic risk-taking, involvement in community/church service, involvement in school activities, involvement in sports both within and outside of the school setting, Grade Point Average (GPA), and class rank.

Your college experience also needs to provide the varied academic base to allow you to successfully maneuver the rapid change, the unpredictable trends of the future, which include multiple job and career changes that you will face in the work place in the 21st Century. Thinking skills, varied experiences, both written and oral communication skills, and interdisciplinary learning (not just within broad areas such as science, but of all areas of study) are the keys, in most cases, rather than specialization. The work place of the 21st Century demands total-package thinkers.

The college countdown—for parents

The *College Countdown* will provide your family with a framework that can be customized to fit your teen and your family. But teens have to do their part also. They need to have the basic skills to not only do their high school course work, but also move onto college. A caveat: The *College Countdown* is a tool for your family, but is not a magic pill for teens and/or families who don't care. This process is fun, but requires work on everyone's part.

You still need to be advocates for your teen in high school. If that has been your pattern all along, now is not the time to stop. If you haven't been an advocate before, now is the time to start. Our kids shouldn't have to fight for appropriate levels of academic opportunities (including properly trained teachers). That is our job as parents and educators.

It is our job to provide our students with a variety of experiences and skills in high school. Colleges assume that students have acquired them before they reach their doors. Research into career areas and the needed thinking skills and college investigation needs to start in the high school freshman year, or before. Imbedded in this process is also the scholarship search process. At the high school setting, parents need to ensure that our students have the very best, highest level academic offerings possible and a well-rounded experience fleshed out with involvement in church/community, after-school activities and sports.

During the summer, if possible, encourage and enable your student to be able to take part in programs that are out of the ordinary for your teen. Examples are employment in career goal areas, your state's Governor's School, Fine Arts Academies, university pre-college and/or pre-professional programs. Try and find experiences out of state if possible. Universities view successfully completed out-of-state experiences as a good indicator of academic risk-taking and forecast of a student's success in college.

High schools and middle schools need to provide top flight courses which will allow our students to stretch and fly academically at all levels. We also need to provide for some nuts and bolts things that will allow our students to be students. There is nothing worse for a student than to have to forego a normal high school activity because someone didn't put quite enough planning into the master schedule. Examples of this conflict would be the prom the weekend before or in between the two AP/IB exam weeks. Since these test dates are known for up to three years in advance, there really isn't a good reason for the conflict.

We also need to ensure that each of our students, especially within the same family, are treated as individuals - they are not clones!

Sometimes it helps before a teen enters a new level or building to have a meeting with the principal and counselors to discuss the student's strengths and limitations. The goal of the meeting is to plan as a partnership how to further strengthen and enhance the educational experiences for this child.

- *Counsel your teen to take as strong a curriculum as possible without overachieving. For some teens this will mean working as hard as possible to get all Cs. For others it will mean including upper-level, college credit and AP/IB courses early in their high school careers. It will only help in the college and scholarship search.*
- *If your high school has a parent academic advocacy group, get active!*
- *Become very familiar and friendly with your teen's principal, class principal and counselors. The lines of communication need to be very open, constructive, and candid. If your teen receives support services from any specialized resource teacher such as in the area of disability and/or gifted education, work with that person to best help your teen. Stay involved all four years.*
- *Encourage your student to seek out summer programs and volunteer/employment opportunities in areas that will give insight into possible career choices. Great examples are part time jobs in an area of interest, pre-college university programs and mentoring relationships.*
- *Start the college search procedure during the freshman year.*
- *Look for opportunities to qualify for your state's Governor's school, Fine Arts Academy, college summer institutes in science, medicine, math and/or writing and other academic experiences whose admissions are also competition-based.*
- *Without truly justifiable reasons, don't let anyone talk you into, or out of, curriculum choices.*
- *Early in the year, initiate and then continue a constant dialogue with your teen's teachers.*
- *Question a learning situation if it just doesn't feel right.*

Become and then continue to be a strong advocate for your teen at the high school level. Even seniors need a bit of help now and then!

The College Countdown—the book

The thoughts, the timeline and the checklists included in *The College Countdown* are meant to only provide a basic structure for you and your family to use. To play the game successfully, you will need to personalize the checklists to fit your individual strengths, weaknesses, interests and needs.

As you work with this book, you will see that on the surface, it appears that this book is written for only high-achieving students. This book is based on the assumption that if you plan for top choices, everything else will fall into place much easier. Every student is different - in strengths and weaknesses; therefore *The College Countdown* is a book to be customized (by choices) by every college-bound teen and family. No matter how you customize the process, it does require hard work. Think of *The College Countdown* as the cookbook for the college application process - to use differing bits and pieces as you go along as you conjure your own unique recipe to college.

Just as each teen is different, how each family handles the division of labor of the process is different. For some families, the teen handles most of the work and the parents act as "reminders" and sounding boards. In other families, the parents do a lot of the groundwork and the teen finishes up the process. As many families as there are in this game at any one time, there are that many methods of physically dividing the work.

Remember what is best for you and your family is what works best with your workload, your personality and your family's dynamics. What works for one family might not work for you.

—Jill F. VonGruben

Praise for *Taming the Paper Monster: The College Game (and it Starts in 8th Grade)*

by Jill F. VonGruben

Having worked with high school students for over twenty years in the field of motivation and goal setting, I can overwhelmingly recommend *Taming the Paper Monster* for students and their parents. Many students are great dreamers, but not all of them have the tools to work toward their goals. This guide gives them a start to finish the road map in charting their own path. Bravo!

MARK SHARENBROICH
Author, Emmy-winner, Award-winning Filmmaker
Motivational Speaker throughout North America

Traditionally the most daunting and frustrating activity a student and family sets out to accomplish is the college search. Anything that can minimize the anxious time is appreciated. Having a carefully planned guide is a tremendous asset. VonGruben's *Taming the Paper Monster* accomplishes this on many levels. It's a must for parents!

ROBERT E. NAGLE
Chairperson, Pupil Personnel Services
Floral Park Memorial High School,
Sewanhaka Central High School District
Floral Park, Long Island, New York

Taming the Paper Monster should be on the night table of every parent who is helping their adolescent get through the college admissions process. It is one of the most user friendly resource guides for families I have ever seen in 25 years as a counselor/guidance supervisor. Jill VonGruben has chosen a format that is concise, easy to access, yet the book is comprehensive in scope.

Taming the Paper Monster walks us through the eighth grade to post high school with checklists, sample resumes, and therapeutic tips on dealing with the emotional roller coaster from late in junior year through May of the senior year.

Clearly, this is a new approach to helping parents and students deal with the anxiety of college admission issues. It is a most refreshing effort.

RON GIANCOLA
Chairman of the Guidance Department
Mineola High School,
Garden City, Long Island, New York

During my thirty-five years in education, the past twenty-one as a high school principal, I have reviewed materials designed to help parents cope with the college application process. I believe that VonGruben's *Taming the Paper Monster* will take the stress out of the process. The format is interesting, easy to follow and very user friendly. The book belongs in every school library and guidance office reference section.

LEON BECKERMAN, PH.D.
Educational Consultant
Eastport, Long Island, New York

Taming the Paper Monster is beautifully told and organized for teens and parents to keep a record of all the "stuff" that goes into this intense process. VonGruben had made the process as painless as possible. This practical, down-to-earth guide helps families successfully work their way through the confusing process of college selection and admission beginning in the 8th grade and continuing through the first year of college.

Taming is so practical that I have recommended the book to parents in the parent education classes I conduct and to teachers in the staff development classes I teach.

DR. SALLY WALKER
Executive Director of the Illinois Association of Gifted Children
Author of Survival Guide for Parents of Gifted Kids

Co-author of Making Memories: A Parent Portfolio
Co-author of Teaching Young Gifted Children in the Regular Classroom

VonGruben's *Taming the Paper Monster* helps students and parents prepare for college, meet deadlines and avoid the pitfalls and problems along the way and complete a successful first year of study.

"Timeline Critical for College Prep," *by Lindsay Gladstone*
The Star, *The Sun-Times Co., Chicago*

If preparing for college is a maze of confusing forms and procedures, Jill VonGruben's book, *Taming the Paper Monster*, will help you cut through red tape like a hot knife glides through butter. Unlike other books of this type, *Taming* will benefit both adolescents and their parents. Filled with anecdotes, forms, dates and reminders of "what's due with", this book offers realistic advice for playing the college game with gusto! Buy it for your college-bound teen…and yourself!

JAMES R. DELISLE, PH.D.
Professor and Teacher, Kent State University
Co-author of The Gifted Kids Survival Guide: A Teen Handbook

VonGruben's *Taming the Paper Monster's* popularity is based on factual information presented from a parents' perspective. As such, it holds a special appeal for parents facing the college admission challenge.

DR. DAN EDWARDS
Principal Lafayette High School
Rockwood School District, St. Louis County, Missouri
Renaissance Educational Foundation Advisory Board Member
Jostens-Renaissance National Trustee Board Member
Chairperson of the Heartland Renaissance Association

Within a few days of receiving a copy of *Taming the Paper Monster*, we were conducting a series of meetings for school counselors. We put the copy on a table of items to share. We were asked by many of those in attendance how they could obtain a copy of this publication. We know many of those who attended were going to purchase copies of their own.

Many parents could find this information useful as they plan to send their son/daughter to post secondary education.

WILLARD WORTS
Supervisor, Guidance Services
Department of Elementary & Secondary Education
State of Missouri

The search for the right college or university, the program that best meets the student's needs, the application process and the search for scholarships are just a few of the traumatic issues facing parents and students. Schools provide assistance but much of the burden is on the family, parent and student.

Taming the Paper Monster is a practical guide for parents and students to help prepare them for these challenges. It is a practical step-by-step approach that takes the family through the planning process for high school, the search for colleges, scholarships and through all the other potential roadblocks that one might face leading up to this important decision. It is certainly a book that I wish I had had in planning for my children as they entered high school and they began their search for colleges. Not only is it an excellent guide for parents and students, it provides valuable information and guidance for educators as well.

JOHN R. OLDANI, ED.D.
Superintendent of Schools, Rockwood School District
St. Louis Country, Missouri

We have used *Taming the Paper Monster* as a resource with parents, students, and teachers at the intermediate, middle school, and high school grade levels. The book provides practical and very helpful information for parents who want to make the right decisions and do the correct things in order to get their child into the best college possible. I would highly recommend it to anyone with a student or child approaching the college years!

KATHY PECKRON, PH.D.
Director of Curriculum, Rockwood School District
St. Louis County, Missouri

To Oliver and Virginia who saw the potential from the very beginning and set the stage for it all to happen. To Bill Keegan, Jr., my agent, who saw the potential and guided it to the next step. To Nancy Mikhail at McGraw-Hill who made it her project also.

To my family for putting up with the vast amount of paper, phone calls, drafts and weird dinners. To my husband, David, who put up with all of us. In addition, most importantly to Kristen and Tracy who were the testing grounds and pilot projects for this book and who took us in such wonderfully divergent directions.

To all of these friends, I send my profound thanks and gratitude.

I dedicate this book to other families involved in the journey.

Acknowledgments

To my many long-suffering friends who listened, provided
and were readers of this manuscript. To the new friends I r
the way each of who gave invaluable advice and support. T
members of my writers' group who cheered me through th
To my daughter, Tracy, for agreeing to do help with the be
work and producing it during her stressed-out Junior year.

To the multitudes of families who shared the stories of thei
—both good and bad. To the many college admission direc
reps who so willingly shared tips and tricks, because their g
was to have great kids succeed no matter what their final c
college turned out to be. To Miami University in Oxford, C
their Western College Interdisciplinary Studies Program. To
University in New Orleans. To Truman State University. To
daughters' advisors and teachers who helped them through
process. To Sally, SMAF, Laura, Judi, Cris, Hillary, Susan, I
Kathy, Vivian, Jim, Pam, Jean, Mary, the two John's in Roc
the two Kim's, Dennis, Bob, Ron and Leon in Long Island,
Rochelle, Pauline, Dan, Steve, Gail, Greg, Sue, Karen, Joyce
the PEGS family who show that everything is possible with
work and support, Sherry, and Rachel; all who gave me hel
back and encouragement. To Cathe, Mike, Dana, Sean, Alis
Lindsay, Jennifer, Misty, Harrison High in Georgia, John in
Mary, Evelyn, Anne, Judson, Kevin and Toni who keep me
To Marie who guided the first stumbling steps at book proc
To my special friends in a certain southern state who cheere
from afar.

Chapter 1

On Your Mark

The Survival Skills—Having What It Takes

- ✔ Study, study, study
- ✔ Get organized
- ✔ Blood, sweat and tears
- ✔ Risks...you don't always have to think twice
- ✔ Write until your hands fall off
- ✔ Speak until your voice is hoarse

Study, study, study

Up until now, you've heard about the importance of working hard about a million times. Well, now it's serious. This sounds simple—you're in school, you're supposed to study. Maybe you've been doing a good job up until now—maybe you haven't. Maybe you study well without being reminded—maybe you don't.

Nevertheless, starting with high school (and earlier for specific courses), the academic choices you make now and the grades you get begin to count toward admission to college.

In addition, businesses are starting to ask for school records and other high school academic information as part of their hiring practices. I know, you're thinking, "businesses? jobs? career? I haven't even gone to the prom yet!" However, do you want to rely on your parents forever? It sounds nice, but your parents probably won't let that happen. Besides, you probably will want to work during high school or even during your summers off. Therefore, the importance of good school records may come sooner than you think. In addition, this is important in your post-college job application process. It's not enough just to have a high school diploma; businesses want to see the quality and strength of your high school experience.

Get organized

Part of studying is not just the physical and mental act of studying, but also the skills of organization and time management. Keeping your life organized will help you keep track of assignments, deadlines, and when you are supposed to be at study groups. Time management skills will allow you to divide your time for each course and project so that you will be able to get them all done and completed. Good time management skills may also very well be the key to having a social life.

This book will help you get organized and manage your time more efficiently as you begin preparing for the college admissions process. If you are having general organization and time management problems, there are a number of books, including daily planners, that can help you get it together. Also, don't forget your teachers and guidance counselors. They are there to help guide you, offer suggestions, and direct you to outside resources.

Don't underestimate the importance of having these skills under your belt. When you're in college, you won't have the luxury of a parent or a teacher hounding you to make sure that you complete all of your assignments on time and prepare for exams. If you get into the habit of studying well now, not only will it help you get through high school successfully, good study skills will also become one of your basic survival skills for college.

It's a partnership

In an ideal world, the high school experience and the college search experience should be a partnership between the teen, the parent(s) and the school. Later the partnership should include the college admission reps from your top choices.

What happens when there is a missing piece to the partnership? It makes the journey a lot longer and a lot more stressful.

YOU are the most vital member of the partnership. Without your complete cooperation, this entire process will fall apart.

If, for whatever reason, you don't have parental support—find a trusted adult to act as your mentor. It can be a teacher, a counselor, a pastor or a relative. Go find someone to act as your support structure and your sounding board.

If the high school is the missing piece in your college search process, the job can still be done. It will mean that you will have to work harder on your own.

By the time you get to your top colleges, those admissions reps are there to help you. All you have to do is ask.

Blood, sweat, and tears

You may be used to your parents' complaining that you spend too much time with your friends, in front of the television, or on the phone. Believe it or not, their constant reminders are good for you. In fact, you're probably used to hearing their complaining. In fact, you may secretly rely on it. Here's news. No one at college will serve as your personal warning bell. Just like with study skills, there will be no one breathing down your neck or looking over your shoulder pushing you to do well in college. So why not start now by learning to work hard on your own?

Some high schools have moved to a differentiated scheduling system. There are several configuration types, but they all allow greater student choice and mimic college schedules. Since their schedules differ every day, students use planners or calendars to keep track of schedules and assignments. These differentiated scheduling models help students to learn time management skills very early in their high school careers.

Remember, high school and college should not just be about your slaving over books. Equally important are the experiences and the activities that you participate in outside of the classroom. In high school, these activities may include sports, school plays, or volunteer work. In college your options mushroom: theater productions, author readings, guest lectures, school newspaper, and more. College outside of the classroom should take your world and expand it beyond your wildest dreams.

How many times have you left a class after a test and said, "But I knew it when I was studying?" How many times have you looked up at the clock and realized you haven't covered even a portion of the material—and the test is tomorrow morning?

If any of this sounds familiar, it's time to work on study and time management skills. Up through 12th grade, you're in class most of the time with the same schedule every day. In fact, the sound of the class bell is probably engrained in your head. Your homework is usually used as reinforcement for what you learned during the day. Time management comes into play only if you are juggling after-school activities and homework. If you paid attention in class and did your couple of hours of homework every night, you could still find time to watch Letterman or Leno.

College is different. You're typically in class for only 12 to 15 hours per week. The rest is on your own. The tried-and-true guideline is that a college student should spend 2 hours of independent study time outside of class for every credit hour. That's typically a minimum of 30 hours per week to study on your own.

One way to help you get a better handle on time management is to buy one of the dozens of daily planners that are on the market. You can find them in your local bookstore, drug store, stationary store, or even at your supermarket.

In college, your independent study a.k.a. homework is not for reinforcement of what has already been taught, but to study new material.

Picture yourself for a moment in Shakespeare 101. You have to read 100 pages of Hamlet in 3 days. But you also have to read the first 4 chapters on inflation vs. deflation in your macroeconomics class. What do you do? No, your dorm monitor is not going to knock on your door and make sure that you have all of your work done. Remember, college is different from high school. So, how are you going to manage it all?

1. **Keep a positive attitude,** even when it gets tough. Is it harder for some kids than others? Of course, but if you stick with it, you will conquer the assignment, the course, the semester, your degree.

2. **Get organized.** For some, that means keeping a daily planner. For others, it can be managed with a little pocket spiral notebook. Whatever it is, stick with it. Write everything down—your assignments, your club meetings, your games, and the times you have blocked out for homework.

3. Discover what your best **learning style** in each subject is and then use those techniques in studying. If you learn best by writing the information down, then make outlines and notes of your reading material. If you absorb more by listening, tape your lectures and then work from your notes and the tapes. Get as many of your assigned reading books on tape if available, then you can read along as you listen and learn the material more easily.

If you are more of a visual learner, then draw diagrams, timelines and charts to help you analyze and then remember the information. Draw cartoons—whatever it takes to help make learning easier, better, and fun.

4. As you learn your best learning style, pay attention to what **study environment** is best for you. For some, it means perfect silence with no distractions. For others, it means background music. For some, it means having the television on. But, also, keep in mind that you will most likely have a roommate. You need to respect his/her study environment needs, also. Work out a schedule for the room and/or the sound.

5. **Set limits for yourself.** Don't try to do it all at once. Break up your study time with exercise, your favorite reruns, or even a scoop of your favorite ice cream. Add some variety. Break up English with math, and so forth.

Studies show that students can't work efficiently for 12 or more straight hours. Forty-five to 60 minute blocks seem to work best. If you have trouble either breaking every hour—or are having too much fun breaking—set a time for yourself so you can get back to studying.

6. **Prepare for class—before** class. Bring your books and your notes. Be ready with questions and to join in the discussions. Participate.

7. **Work on learning to think critically.** In college, it's usually not enough to just feed back information to the professor—you will need to apply the knowledge. This means memorizing is not enough. You have to understand what you're reading.

8. Continually **review** during the semester. Again, do this in small chunks of material. You'll retain the informa-

tion so that you'll truly know and understand the material (so you can remember and apply it for much more than tomorrow's exam). Constant review during the semester will make finals week so much easier. Because you've already learned the material—you'll just have to refresh yourself. What do you review? One of the things is your class notes. Be neat, so you won't waste time deciphering your own handwriting. Tape-record lectures if you need to. More notes aren't necessarily better. Organized notes that show the relationships among ideas are the best.

9. **Break reading assignments into short blocks**—using section headings as a gauge. You'll learn faster and retain the information longer.

10. **Get some sleep.** Sleep can be your greatest study ally. Sleep deprivation goes beyond hindering learning—it stops it.

TIME OUT

Study groups are a very effective tool and can be a great of way of getting to know your peers. One hallmark of a good study group is one that meets regularly, not just the night before exams.

Risks...you don't always have to think twice

In getting ready for college, why would anyone not want to play it academically safe?

Educational or academic risk-takers are those who want to try something new and to learn something new. Colleges look for them, because those students become the most rewarding ones to the universities. Eventually, they become the researchers, the inventors, and the best teachers.

What are risks you can take during high school? Make the choice of a harder course over one where you know you'll do better. Try out for a play or work backstage. Go out for a sports team. Run for student council. Go where you haven't been before. Go where—for you—it's not safe and secure.

Learning to take risks will make you a well-rounded individual. Learning to take risks is what college is all about. A true college experience is not about being safe and secure academically. Another way of looking at taking risks is asking the questions, "Why?" and, "What If?" If you incorporate questioning into your daily life, you are building the basis for a strong risk-taking pattern.

Risk taking, by definition, is uncomfortable. You're doing something new. You may not be successful. But risk taking also assumes you are taking initiative. Being able to be self-motivated, to ask questions, and to find the answers that you are looking for is the pattern of true learning. This pattern will bring you the wide base of knowledge that is so vital to college success.

PARENTS CORNER

In a few short years, your children won't be at home. If they've never had practice in making good decisions, how will they survive when they are on their own? It's a recipe for disaster. Your teen might need your encouragement and support to take risks in academic and interest choices. Our teens learn best by example. They will more likely become risk-takers if they see their parents taking risks, whether in business, or in new learning experiences. Discuss your risk taking and the results, both the successes and failures. Talk about how you make decisions.

Reading...for fun?

When you think of reading, do you think of the comics in the daily or weekend paper? Or do you think of an encyclopedia that's bigger than you are?

Reading is the cornerstone of all learning. During high school, it will become a much larger portion of what you do for your classes. By the time college rolls around, reading will consume almost every waking hour. There will be hundreds of pages to read a week in not just one, but several subjects.

With an expanding reading base, you will be incorporating learning into every day. Make reading a passion in your life. If you read for fun, not only will you gain the strong vocabulary needed for college admission, you will be building a broad base of knowledge—and knowledge is power.

How does reading build your vocabulary? First of all, you are exposed to a wide variety of words and usages. Secondly, you will be introduced to a slew of unfamiliar words. What should you do with those words? This is where your dictionary comes in. Have it with you when you are reading or studying. Look up words that you don't recognize or understand in a particular context. It's a good study habit to write the words down (index cards work well) and also write the definition on the card.

Success on standardized college admissions tests strongly depends on your reading and vocabulary skills. One of the best ways to prepare for the SAT or ACT tests is to read not just during the year you plan to take these tests, but for many years beforehand. These tests will refer to your reading since you were a small child.

How do you cope? Get in habit of reading now if reading isn't a normal part of your life. How do you start? Find a book that covers a subject that interests you and then build from there. Vary your reading between fiction and nonfiction, between the classics and current popular titles. With the exception of language arts courses in college, most of your required reading will be in nonfiction.

What if reading is difficult for you? What if you read very slowly? What if you can't remember what you just read? Ask for help from your parents or from your guidance counselor, who may have some reading comprehension workshops or programs to help you. And practice—the more you read, the easier it will become. If you're having trouble retaining information when you read, but learn better by hearing, try reading along with the book on tape. More and more literature is now available on cassette tapes and CDs.

This might be a good time to take a speed-reading course. Reading courses like this will not only teach you how to read faster with greater comprehension, but, also, how to distinguish those materials that can be covered by speed-reading from other materials that are meant to be studied more slowly and carefully.

Colleges expect a certain volume of reading to occur in a student's life before he/she gets there. They will look to see that you have read a variety of works, from fiction to nonfiction, from the classics to popular bestsellers.

PARENTS CORNER

How do you know which books your child should begin reading? You can talk with his/her English teacher, guidance counselor, or even talk with the school librarian. In addition, you can often find recommended reading lists at your local public library.

Remember, reading a wide variety of works allows you to improve your vocabulary painlessly. Look up words you don't know or understand. Keep track of them to review from time to time. By reading great writing, you become a better writer—not only in vocabulary, but also in style and structure. Also, if you are well-read before you get to college, chances are you will be assigned one of the books you read on your own.

The following is an abbreviated list of authors recommended by colleges across the country. Add to these as much nonfiction as you can from autobiographies, biographies, history, economics, science and philosophy.

For specific lists of suggested or recommended readings, contact the colleges you are interested in. Books of reading lists of a variety of schools across the country are available at libraries and bookstores.

You will notice that even this abbreviated list of authors is quite long. You can't read all of these the summer before you go to college, so start now.

Acevedo Diaz, Edvardo
Alearia, Ciro
Angelou, Maya
Asturias, Miguel Angel
Austin, Jane
Baraka, Imamu Amiri (LeRoi Jones)
Baroja, Pia
Beckett, Samuel
The Bible
Brecht, Bertolt
Bronte, Charlotte
Bronte, Emily
Brooks, Gwendolyn
Brown, William Wells
Calderon, Pedro
Carroll, Lewis
Cather, Willa
Cela, Camilo Jose
Cervantes, Miguel de
Chaucer, Geoffrey
Chekhov, Anton
Chopin, Kate
Crane, Stephen
Dante
Darwin, Charles
Defoe, Daniel
Dickens, Charles
Douglass, Frederick
Dubois, W.E..B.
Ellison, Ralph
Emerson, Ralph Waldo
Equiano, Olaudah
Faulkner, William
Fitzgerald, F. Scott
Fuentos, Carlos
Gallegos, Romula
Goethe, Johann von
Golding, William
HD (Hilde Doolittle)
Hamilton, Edith
Hardy, Thomas
Hawthorne, Nathaniel
Hemingway, Ernest
Homer
Hurston, Zora Neale
Hughes and Bontemps
Hughes, Langston
Huxley, Aldous
Ibsen, Henrik
Icaza, Jorges
James, Henry
Johnson, James Weldon
Joyce, James
Kafka, Franz
Larson, Nella
Lawrence, D.H.
Lewis, C.S.
Lewis, Sinclair
Lorca, Federico Garcia
Lorde, Audrey
Malcom X
Mann, Thomas
Marlowe, Christopher
Garcia Marquez, Gabriel
Melville, Herman

Miller, Arthur
Milton, John
Milosz, Czeslaw
Moliere
Montale, Eugenio
Moore, Marianne
Morrison, Toni
O'Neill, Eugene
Oates, Joyce Carol
Orwell, George
Paton, Alan
Paz, Octavio
Plato
Poe, Edgar Allen
Purdy, James
Quiroga, Horacio
Rulfo, Juan
Sabato, Ernesto
Sanchez, Sonia
Salinger, J.D.
Scott, Sir Walter
Shakespeare, William
Shaw, George Bernard
Shelley, Mary
Steinbeck, John
Swift, Jonathan
Thoreau, Henry David
Tolstoy, Leo
Twain, Mark
Unamuno, Miguel de
Updike, John
Virgil
Voltaire
Vonnegut, Kurt
Walker, Alice
Walker, Margaret
Welty, Eudora
Wharton, Edith
Whitman, Walt
Wilde, Oscar
Wilder, Thornton
Williams, Tennessee
Wilson, Harriet
Woods, Donald
Woolf, Virginia
Wright, Richard

★ ★ ★ ★ ★ ★ ★ ★ ★ ★ ★ ★ ★ ★ ★ ★ ★

Trudy: a student profile

Trudy wanted to go to a selective college out west. She applied and was rejected. Why? Because while her math scores were within acceptance range, her verbal scores were low.

What did she do? She applied and was accepted to a local nonselective college. But she didn't give up her dream and stop there. She asked a friend, famous for her reading habits, for help. They discussed Trudy's goals and her reading list up until then. They came up with a list of authors and titles Trudy would need to read to build her up.

Trudy started reading constantly on her own. She looked up all the words in the dictionary she did not recognize. It took a year-and-a-half of concentrated work, but she reapplied to her first choice school and was admitted as a transfer student.

Not everyone is as driven and motivated as Trudy was to work independently in a concentrated time period. It's better if you build your reading list and vocabulary slowly over time. Trudy will be the first to tell you that.

Write until your hand falls off

If reading is how you obtain the majority of your knowledge in school, then writing is the major way you transmit knowledge back to your teachers.

"How to Write" is taught in your language arts classes. Practicing those writing methods should be as much of your daily life as reading should be. The more you write, the easier it will become, and the better you will become. Once again, practice is the key.

As you get more actively involved in the college admissions process, you'll find that good writing skills will play a key role when it comes to putting together the college admissions essays. These essays will give colleges a true glimpse of yourself—and it could be your opportunity to showcase your writing skills. Remember, writing will be your main form of communication throughout your collegiate and professional career.

TIME OUT

Most multiple choice exams test only a raw knowledge base. Writing essays and papers test critical thinking and application of that knowledge. And this is what college is all about—truly knowing the subject matter. This is what your career(s) will require—applied knowledge.

Writers are self-made. Don't think that you don't have what it takes to write well. Remember, if you can learn to play basketball, you can put the pen to paper and do it well. If your school does not require writing intensive curricula, demand it of yourself. Keep a journal. Keep a list of new words you've come across. Write about anything and everything. The key is to practice consistently.

What colleges want in your writing

- ✔ Need a thesis statement: A.k.a., What position are you defending?
- ✔ Needs to be well organized.
- ✔ Answers the question in its entirety in a concise manner.
- ✔ to be Well written.
- ✔ Use good grammar.
- ✔ Check your spelling.
- ✔ The piece needs to flow.
- ✔ Needs a valid conclusion.

PARENTS CORNER

What will colleges look for in your child's writing? Their thoughts should be well organized, concise, to the point, and most importantly, *grammatically correct*. Pick up any of the dozens of grammar books available in bookstores for your son or daughter. Good grammar skills are like time management skills—they are the kind that they will use for life. You can pick up two extremely helpful McGraw-Hill titles: *Rules of Thumb: A Guide for Writers* and *Schaum's Outline of English Grammar.*

Speak until your voice is hoarse

Good oral presentation skills are an extension of good writing skills. Students not only have to present themselves well on paper, but also in face-to-face encounters. Public speaking can be difficult for some. You need to be dynamic and succinct so you can gain and hold your audience's attention. But it is a skill that can be learned and then honed with practice. Good oral communication skills are important for your professional life as well. From giving speeches at conferences and seminars to simply talking in front of your managers and colleagues, being able to speak confidently in public will be essential to your daily work life.

Basic skills are now taught in freshman courses (some of which are required courses). Presentation skills are also enhanced by class discussions. To become more comfortable with your presentation skills, practice in front of a mirror with a tape recorder. If you have access to a video camera, this is an almost ideal practice situation. Watch your tapes several times and then keep perfecting your delivery style.

Highlights

- ★ Time management skills will help you not only do better in school but will allow you to have a social life as well.
- ★ Risk taking and learning go hand in hand. Think about taking a harder course in high school or try going out for a team.
- ★ Reading is the connection of all learning. Not only will it build your vocabulary, you'll be better prepared for the all important PSATs, SATs and the host of other college admission exams.
- ★ Learn how to express yourself. Writers and speakers are not born. Practice, practice, practice.

Chapter 2

Get Set

The College Game Starts in 8th Grade

- ✔ Jump in head first, now
- ✔ Goooooaaal!
- ✔ Get some class
- ✔ The class rank game
- ✔ Gearing up for the big game

Jump in head first, now

Eighth grade. Doesn't preparing for college really start during the junior and senior years of high school?

No, it really started the first day you entered school. It begins with your attitude toward school and learning. But for our purposes, the process starts here because during second semester you will be filling out your schedule for 9th grade. You don't have till next August or September to think about 9th grade—*the time is now.*

Often, we are told, it is what you do in high school that matters. That's where the grades count and that middle school isn't that important in comparison. That's wrong. You need to work hard in middle school, especially 8th grade to establish good study patterns and to obtain the necessary academic background so you can do well in 9th grade and beyond. If you leave 8th grade with poor study and time management skills and habits, it's going to make 9th grade success very difficult.

PARENTS CORNER

College planning in middle school? Something just for the top students? According to the National Association of College Admissions Counselors, the American School Counselors Association, the National Association for Student Financial Aid Administrators and the National Association of Independent Colleges and Universities, college preparation and information needs to be part of every junior high student's experience.

Now is the time to get your child to start thinking about his/her strengths and weaknesses in school. This will help him/her to begin thinking about long-term college decisions such as which courses to take and what major to pursue.

It's never too early to start the college process. Why? What do colleges look for? The following table tries to quantify the decision parameters of colleges. Student activities, essays, and interviews need to be added to the information below to complete the decision-making structure. Keep in mind that these are very general parameters and differ over time and from school to school.

Getting those top test scores won't happen overnight, even with a test prep class. They can only be gained through years of hard work and study. It can't wait until your high school junior year, so start now.

Type of College	Combined SAT Range	Composite ACT Range	Acceptance Rate	Class Position
Nonselective/ Noncompetitive	800 or less	20 or less	90%	N/A
Less selective/ Less competitive	900 or less	21 or less	45%–90%	N/A
Selective/Competitive	900 or more	21 or more	49%–80%	Top 50%
Highly selective/ Highly competitive	1100 or more	25 or more	36%–69%	Top 33%
Most selective/ Most competitive	1200 or more	27 or more	11%–55% (most under 28%)	Top 15%

Financial Aid Already? Parents, it's not too early to start thinking about college finances and financial aid. As your child prepares academically for the next four years, you need to start your own four-year financial plan for college. You should begin by consulting your financial planner and/or tax professional about your family's financial picture with regard to tax planning and college financial aid. At this point, there are no deadlines to worry about. Right now, you need to start looking at the how's and the why's. Become informed. More about college finance will be discussed later in this book.

Gooooaaal!

As you work with your parents and guidance counselor on planning class schedules, use this time to work on setting academic goals. Why? Because going to high school is not just to take up four years of your life. You want those four years to mean something to you and do something for you. Maybe you want your high school experience to enable you to attend an Ivy League school. Maybe you want your high school experience to pave the way so that you can play professional sports. Maybe you want your high school experience to allow you to become a teacher, a chemist, or a business owner.

You can't achieve any of these objectives without having a plan. And to make a plan you need to set some concrete goals for yourself. Before you can set goals, you need to do some exploring within yourself. The following form is a list of a few of the questions you might want to ask yourself. Answer them on paper and give yourself plenty of time to think and analyze yourself.

1. What are your study habits? (Where do you study? When do you study? Do you study in groups?

2. What are your time management skills? (Do you find yourself constantly cramming for tests? Do you do your homework at the last minute, or worse, not at all? Do you keep a daily planner? Are your parents and teachers constantly scolding you for not being prepared for school?)

3. What are your academic strengths? Weaknesses? (Are you better in English than in math? Would you rather read about the U.S. Civil War than amebas?)

4. How would you describe yourself? Check the following traits that apply to you, but don't limit your description to this list.)

   Organized
   Articulate
   Shy
   Pay attention to details
   A leader
   Motivated
   A numbers person
   Enjoys art and literature
   Athletic

5. Which activities do you enjoy doing most outside of the classroom?

(Continued)

6. What are some of the things/people that matter to you the most (your friends, how well you do in school, being accepted by your peers, your parents, your privacy, your CDs...)?

7. What do you wish you could improve about yourself (that you are more outgoing, perform better in school, etc.)?

8. What do you enjoy most learning about?

9. Have you given any thought to what you would like to major in college? (If you haven't, don't worry about it! Most college students don't know themselves!)

10. What are your biggest fears/concerns about college and the whole process?

Once you have answered these questions, think about setting some goals for yourself:

- *If you've discovered that you really do like word problems and earth science, why not take on outside related interests? For instance, join a math club or read about home science experiments. In other words, harness and develop these interests. If you like music, but don't know how to play an instrument, take a lesson. If you have wonderful communication skills, think about taking on more of a leadership role in any of the clubs or sports you already belong to.*
- *If you know that you want to do something with computers after college, why not spend some time logging on, pick up a computer book, or visit your guidance counselor and talk about your interest? Often, your teachers and counselors are your best resource to put you directly in touch with the people and businesses that can help you develop your interests.*
- *If you have absolutely no idea what you want to do once you're in college, don't worry. Technically, you don't have to decide until the end of your sophomore year in college. But, if you're worried that you haven't done well in school up to this point, now is the time to crack open those books and get organized. Examine how you schedule your time and how you are organized as a person. (Are you having difficulty balancing all of the homework you have for your classes? Are you overburdened with papers, tests, and assignments that are due?)*
- *If you're ready to set some goals (e.g., I want to do better in algebra, I want to raise my grade in history), write them down and think about what it will take to accomplish them in terms of knowledge, time, and resources.*
- *Organize your goals in order of their level of importance to you.*
- *Examine the factors that will help you or hinder you in achieving your goals. Are you too shy to join a sport or a club? Do you lack the finances to say, buy a horse?*

Now you're ready to make a plan. Create a timeline for when you want to achieve your goals. You should do this for each goal and then put them all together to make a master plan. Now, add your goals and timelines to your planner or calendar.

TIME OUT

As with any good plan, you have to return, revisit, and revise. Things outside of your control will change what you can accomplish at a certain time of your life. A new interest or ability may come into your life. You will change with age and maturity. How you view the world will change as you read more complex materials and meet new people. Change is good—just make sure you're keeping track of it.

PARENTS CORNER

Get your teen to think about his/her career now. Why? Because he/she can make use of his/her high school years to explore academic areas that will support his/her career interest. How can you get your teen to start exploring career choices? Think about what your teen likes to do outside of the classroom. Does he enjoy writing? Does she spend hours in front of the computer? Whatever the interests are, help your teen explore them further by getting him/her more involved in these areas, getting him/her to read more about their interests, and by talking with your own friends and colleagues who can offer more direction both to you and your teen. Remember, it's best to focus in on an interest that already intrigues your teen.

Career exploration begins with the same questions that you ask yourself for goal setting. The short list is: What do you like to study? What do you like to do? What are your hobbies? There are interest "inventory tests" available through your guidance counselor's office at school. But remember, these results aren't set in stone. Your results may be different the next year around.

Another way to start thinking about possible career choices is to try to match your abilities, your interests, and the values you have about the workplace. Some examples of workplace values might be a job that allows a high degree of creativity, or variety, or a good salary, job security, working outdoors, or working with people.

It's worth the time and effort to analyze yourself throughout your high school and college career so that your workplace Monday mornings will be pleasant experiences. Over time, you, the workplace, and your chosen career will change. If you haven't been taking your "pulse" all along, these changes will catch you off-guard. If you have been taking your personal inventory "pulse," you'll be prepared either to adapt to the change or to take proactive steps to change your choice.

Having an idea of what interests you will assist you in deciding on a college program to pursue, which will in turn lead you to a college choice. Each builds on the other.

TIME OUT

The Campbell Interest and Skill Survey (CISS), which is available at http://www.usnews.com/usnews/nycu/work/wocciss.htm, is an assessment tool that people use to learn about the career that's best suited to their specific skills and interests. The CISS consists of 320 questions and takes less than an hour to complete. Within approximately 3 weeks after you complete the test, you will receive a report that matches your interests with your career options. This could be a great tool to help you guide you into a career area—and perhaps, ultimately, a college choice.

Get some class

At this point, you will have to start thinking about your first year of high school and which classes you want to take in 9th grade. When choosing classes, keep in mind that colleges will carefully examine the courses you take—especially in areas of math, science, and English. You should take as high a level in the classes you choose as you can manage—while also having a varied life outside academics. **BUT,** high school counts—stay away from easy courses. One example is the 9th grade general physical science course. This particular course usually does not count as a high school requirement in the science category. Examine your high school offerings versus what colleges want for in those core areas.

As of this writing, the high school curricula required by the best universities generally require the following core high school courses:

- *4 years English*
- *4 years college prep math (Algebra I and above)*
- *3–4 years of science (including at least 2 lab sciences)*

  Note: make sure one is Biology
- *2–4 years of a single foreign language*
- *3–4 years of social science (history, social studies, etc.)*
- *1 year of fine arts*

These basic requirements should be fleshed out with electives such as computer science and extracurricular activities that will enable you to become a well-rounded student.

★★★★★★★★★★★★★★★★★

Thom: a student profile

Thom transferred into a new school district. He was from a school in which the guidance was of very high quality. He made the assumption that it was the same in his new school. When it was time to make out his four-year plan, Thom had four years of science (including two Advanced Placement science courses), but did not take Biology. He just wasn't interested.

During Thom's junior year as he started to talk with college admissions reps, he discovered that not only would they not take the general science course he took during 9th grade, but he needed to take Biology to be admitted. There was no room left in his schedule for another whole credit (year) class before graduation. He wanted to graduate on time.

What did he do? Thom enrolled in Biology via a university correspondence course and had to do that work while carrying a schedule heavy with Advanced Placement courses. Moral of the story? Make sure every class you take will be accepted by the colleges you consider—yes, even 9th grade classes.

★★★★★★★★★★★★★★★★★

Some states have moved to increase the amount of foreign language courses available to students, starting in junior high. If this is the case in your state, you are ahead of the game.

If you are able to take foreign language courses during junior high, and if you have enough room in your schedule, you may then be able to add a second foreign language in high school.

If your high school offers Latin, this might be an option to take at some point in your secondary career. Why take a "dead" language like Latin? Studying Latin provides the following benefits:

- *An excellent foundation for learning foreign languages*
- *A strong background in grasping grammatical components of the English language (makes reading easier)*

- *Students taking Latin tend to have higher verbal scores on the SAT and ACT college entrance exams*
- *Used in the fields of medicine and law*
- *Exposure to a language and culture that had a major impact on the modern world*

The solid top

How do colleges know if you have taken the easy way out? Admissions Reps feel so strongly about the strength of the core courses that they often refer to them as the "Solid Top 5". Often, scholarship and college applications will ask either you or your high school guidance counseling office to fill in a grid with the courses you have taken each year compared to what the most difficult courses available that year in those subject areas were. Colleges do not expect every student to max out in every area, but what they do look for is a well-rounded student who takes some academic risks. A sample of such a grid is shown in the following form.

COURSE GRID

Core Curriculum	9th Grade Took	9th Grade Top Avail.	10th Grade Took	10th Grade Top Avail.	11th Grade Took	11th Grade Top Avail.	12th Grade Took	12th Grade Top Avail.
English								
Math								
Science								
History/Social Studies								
Foreign Language								

The class rank game

The class rank race is a game played by some students and their parents and is only important to them. It is not the most important thing considered in the selection process by colleges. The choice of an academically challenging and well-rounded education gains more respect than a top class rank.

Here is a mental trick to defuse the Class Rank game: When you first have that 4-year plan completed and in front of you—compute the cumulative Grade Point Average (GPA) if the maximum grades are achieved in each course. Now, you've played the "game" on paper. You don't ever have to play it again. Now go and learn as much as you can.

The Class rank game can also lead to or foster the negative aspects of perfectionism. Being perfect is not what even the best universities are looking for. What universities are looking for are the students who have dreams and are taking the steps to reach those dreams. Colleges are not looking for the parents' dreams, the grandparents' dreams, the guidance counselors' or teachers' dreams, but your own dreams.

The goal for you has to be what is best for you, the individual, not you, so-and-so's daughter or you, so-and-so's grandson. Notice the stress on "individual." What works for you doesn't necessarily work for another. Keeping this in mind will make your college decisions easy to figure out.

Playing the class rank game to win in your senior year by stacking your schedule with weighted grade classes so that you hope to earn a perfect "5" may win that game for you, but you'll lose ground in the eyes of a college admissions rep. The class rank game is considered so destructive that some high schools do not issue class ranks or name Valedictorians or Salutatorians. If you are working at your max and a C average is your top, then you have really won the game. Ignore the students who are making their friends their opponents and giving themselves ulcers at an early age because of class rank. The real game here is doing your best, whatever that is.

The following form displays several versions of the class rank game played by four students. The examples show computing GPA under several conditions including the weighted grade option. The examples are given so you can see how GPAs are computed and so that you, too, can play the game—but only on paper. It's the only place it needs to be played.

COMPUTING GPA (GRADE POINT AVERAGE)

Most schools consider a semester as a one-half credit and assign the following numerical values to letter grades:

A	4
B	3
C	2
D	1
F	0

COMPUTING GPA (GRADE POINT AVERAGE)

One student has taken six 2-semester classes receiving no A's, 1 B and 5 C's.

Letter Grade		Grade Value		Credit		Credit Value Points
B	×	3	×	1	=	3
C	×	2	×	1	=	2
C	×	2	×	1	=	2
C	×	2	×	1	=	2
C	×	2	×	1	=	2
C	×	2	×	1	=	2
				6		13

13 credit value points divided by 6 credits = 2.167 GPA for that year.

COMPUTING GPA (GRADE POINT AVERAGE)

Another student has taken six 2-semester classes receiving no A's, 2 B's and 4 C's.

Letter Grade		Grade Value		Credit		Credit Value Points
B	×	3	×	1	=	3
B	×	3	×	1	=	3
B	×	3	×	1	=	3
C	×	2	×	1	=	2
C	×	2	×	1	=	2
C	×	2	×	1	=	2
				6		15

15 credit value points divided by 6 credits = 2.500 GPA for that year.

A third student has taken six 2-semester classes receiving 3 A's, 2 B's and 1 C.

COMPUTING GPA (GRADE POINT AVERAGE)

A third student has taken six 2-semester classes receiving 3 A's, 2 B's and 1 C.

Letter Grade		Grade Value		Credit		Credit Value Points
A	×	4	×	1	=	4
A	×	4	×	1	=	4
A	×	4	×	1	=	4
B	×	3	×	1	=	3
B	×	3	×	1	=	3
C	×	2	×	1	=	2
				6		20

20 credit value points divided by 6 credits = 3.333 GPA for that year.

COMPUTING GPA (GRADE POINT AVERAGE) WITH WEIGHTED GRADE OPTION

This is an example of computing a GPA with a weighted grade option. This is the same as the previous example, but the student has taken one weighted grade class. Most schools consider a semester as a one-half credit and assign the following numerical values to letter grades:

Weighted Grade Class		Non-weighted Grade Class	
Letter Grade	Grade Value	Letter Grade	Grade Value
A	5	A	4
B	4	B	3
C	3	C	2
D	1(no extra earned)	D	1
F	0	F	0

One student has taken six 2-semester classes receiving 1 weighted grade A', 2 A's, 2 B's and 1 C.

Letter Grade		Grade Value		Credit		Credit Value Points
A	×	5	×	1	=	5
A	×	4	×	1	=	4
A	×	4	×	1	=	4
B	×	3	×	1	=	3
B	×	3	×	1	=	3
C	×	2	×	1	=	2
				6		21

21 credit value points divided by 6 credits = 3.500 GPA for that year.

Gearing up for the big game

You're not even in high school yet and already you are making preparations for college. Below is a grid that explains exactly where you will be going in the next year, depending on whether you are in public or private school.

Public School	Private School
• *If you attend public school in junior high, advancement to high school is automatic as long as you pass the eighth grade. In the spring of your eighth grade, you will be required to take a math placement test and, most likely, an English placement test. The results of these tests will allow proper placement in your math and English classes for 9th grade. You and your parents will be given the scores before it is time to make your schedule out for 9th grade.*	*There are two different transitions to private secondary education. The first transition time is 6th and 7th grades. Students who finish private elementary education enter into the private secondary school selection process during 6th grade for 7th grade entrance. These students will then attend the private secondary school from 7th through 12th grades.*
• *If you attend a traditional junior high/middle school, often you are not given the opportunity to take heavy-duty course work because differentiated curricula are not part of the traditional junior high school/middle school theory. If this has been the case, you will need to do some work on your own.*	*The second traditional transition, usually found in parochial school education, is 8th and 9th grades. Students who finish parochial elementary education enter into either the private or parochial secondary school selection process during 8th grade for 9th grade entrance. These students will then attend the private secondary school from 9th through 12th grades.*

Home Schoolers—a Special Note

The best home schooling programs take the student out of the home into the community for hands-on experiential learning. If this has been your choice, you will need to increase this component in your curricula for high school. Involvement with the community at large becomes vital in your formulation as a college candidate.

Look for mentors in the academic areas in which you excel. You will need to become involved in community projects that bring you in touch with other teens and adults. A home school teen needs a full and meaningful resume even more than a traditionally schooled teen. Validation of your experiences will become vital in your college admissions process. Since your family is your teacher, you will need to look outside your family for contacts that will be able to supply scholastic and character recommendations.

You will need to make sure that your home schooled curriculum matches the expectations of colleges with regard to academic rigor and variety. Courses at a local junior college might provide a solution for a missing foreign language or performing art, for example.

Depending upon which state you live in, there may be standardized testing requirements. If not, ensure that you receive nationally recognized standardized testing throughout your high school years. It will become your responsibility to obtain test dates, test registration packets, etc. Colleges will require objective testing tools.

You can use The College Countdown later in this book to provide you with the timelines and information that colleges will require upon application.

Home School Legal Defense Association

This Web site gives all types of information on home schooling along with a search capability to find home school organizations in your state.

The National Center for Home Education is a division of the Home School Legal Defense Association. Their Web site serves as a national clearinghouse for home schooling information and research.

http://www.hslda.org/nationalcenter/

If you and your parents feel that your standardized achievement scores are not what you think they should be, you'll need to do some independent study. More studying? You are doing a lot, but those test scores could really affect the private high school you get accepted to or the classes you take in public high school. If you feel your vocabulary skills are weak, increase the amount and variety of your outside reading. If you feel your math skills need help, get a math workbook or computer drill program to help beef up your skills.

Remember, the most important skill you can give yourself, at this point, is working well and hard. When you get to 9th grade, you will need to master a great deal of material in a much shorter time than you're used to.

For private/parochial schools, whether you're looking at secondary school in 6th grade or 8th grade, the calendar **To-Do-List** is the same.

Beginning in the 5th and early 6th grades/7th and early 8th grades, gather information. The search and selection process for parochial and private secondary school admissions is very similar to that for college admissions. Visit the schools in which you are interested. Acquire as much information as possible from the, course catalogs, website information, and personal information from alumni and parents. There will often be open houses that provide general information and tours. Personal visit days are encouraged so the student can spend time with current students and go to a couple of classes to get a feel for the campus philosophy.

PARENTS CORNER

During the transition year (6th or 8th grades), a number of steps need to fall into place as you prepare your teen for high school. Here's a quick run-down of things you need to make sure are in order:

Calendar of the Transition Year (6th or 8th Grades)

- Your teen has to take an exploratory test offered in school during late 5th or 7th grades.
- Verify with the high school which specialized admissions test is required by the school(s) and register for the test during the fall.
- Help your teen obtain the necessary amount and type of recommendations requested by the school. Normally these are filed with the application.
- Have your teen complete and file the application as soon as possible in the fall. Depending upon the reputation of the school, spots usually fill in quickly.
- Have elementary school transcripts sent to the school where your teen is applying.
- Complete and file the financial aid application as soon as possible in the fall.
- Schedule your teen's on-campus interview, if one is required, during the designated period, usually between October through December or mid-February.
- Work on the self-examination, goals and career exploration portions of this section that should be part of all 8th grade students' applications.
- Help your teen work to establish personal as well as career goals. In addition, help your child improve test-taking and time management skills. Since a number of entrance exams will begin during this stage (more about this will be discussed in the next section), help your teen prepare by encouraging him/her to read more—this will help him/her develop his/her vocabulary skills.

- Have your teen take the required admissions tests. Verify the date for each required test. Some tests are only offered once while others are offered more than once.
- Respond on time to requests for information made by the school.
- Admissions decisions are usually made and announced in February or March.
- Accepted students must notify the school and secure their place with a deposit by early March or April. The exact deadline will be given to you. If you have applied to more than one school, also notify the schools you are declining.
- Have your teen attend New Student Orientation or meetings held in the spring.

If you plan to attend a private high school, you will need to take one of the entrance exams available:

Independent School Entrance Examination (ISEE)

The ISEE is a more recent independent high school admission test. The ISEE is, in some cases, now accepted in lieu of the SSAT (see below). The Educational Records Bureau administers the test. You may request information and an ISEE Student Guide from the Educational Records Bureau [(800)989-3721] if it is not available from the school itself.

The ISEE is offered for the two traditional transition years. The middle level is given to students who want to transfer into the 6th, 7th, or 8th grades. The upper level test is for students to transfer into the 9th through 12th grades.

The ISEE has four multiple-choice sections that test verbal ability, quantitative ability, reading comprehension, and mathematics achievement. The test sections range from 20 to 40 minutes long. There is also a 30-minute essay.

Secondary School Admission Test (SSAT)

The SSAT is the traditional independent secondary school entrance exam. The Educational Testing Service administers the exam.

The SSAT is offered for the two traditional transition years. The lower level is given to students who want to transfer into the 6th, 7th, or 8th grades. The upper level test is for students to transfer into the 9th through 12th grades.

The SSAT has five multiple-choice sections. Two sections are mathematical tests, one includes synonyms and analogies, and the final test is for reading comprehension. The fifth section is not scored, but is used to test future test questions. All tests run 25 minutes.

Scholastic Testing Service High School Placement Test (HSPT)

The HSPT is a test used primarily by Catholic High Schools. The Scholastic Testing Service administers it. This test is given in the 8th grade for admission into 9th grade high school.

The HSPT has five multiple-choice sections that cover verbal skills, quantitative skills, reading, mathematics and language skills. The basic test runs about 2½ hours. A high school may opt to add one of the following tests to the other five: mechanical aptitude, science, or Catholic religion.

Cooperative Entrance Exam (COOP)

The COOP is a test used for entrance into 9th grade. It is published by CTB/McGraw-Hill.

Thirty percent of the COOP is changed each year, but generally has 7 parts that usually cover sequences, analogies, memory skills, verbal reasoning, reading comprehension, mathematics, and language expression. This test runs about 2¾ hours, but does have a 15-minute break in the middle.

Other individual tests

The above four tests are the primary nationally available secondary entrance exams. Your individual school or Archdiocese may specify their own testing vehicle. You need to verify which test with the individual schools.

Highlights

★ Work out your 9th grade schedule now, keeping in mind what classes will be accepted by colleges. Also, make a rough course plan for the rest of your high school career, based on your 9th grade choices.

★ Parents, begin the Financial Aid process now. Examine your present financial situation and set up an appointment to speak with a financial planner or tax professional.

★ Gooooaaal! No, this isn't a European soccer game, it's your life. Start asking yourself now what your strengths and weaknesses are and what you enjoy learning. These answers will help you map out your high school career and make decision-making a lot easier.

★ Remember this phrase, "Solid Top 5". They are the five core courses that nearly every college will be looking for in your transcript. No matter how many sports, clubs or elective courses you have under your belt, without math, science, English, history, and a foreign language, college admissions people won't waste their time looking any further. These five core courses will almost guarantee you acceptance into that dream college of yours.

★ One thing the college admissions people don't care about is class rank. Don't waste your time worrying about it. The key here is to do your best, take that AP course, and deal with a C+. It will be looked upon much more favorably than Study Hall 101 where you got an A.

★ For students considering private or parochial high school, you need to map out a timeline. There is a process you have to follow, including school tours, recommendations, and even financial aid, much the same as the process for college. Start now and remember, this is excellent practice for junior year when you do it all over again for college.

Chapter 3

Go!

9th Grade—The Clock Starts

- ✔ Get yourself a resume
- ✔ Be a joiner
- ✔ Uncle Sam is calling

It's 9th Grade and it all counts for real now. Use your "survival skills" to build a successful first year in high school. If you do that, you will be laying foundation for a strong bridge to college.

Get yourself a resume

If you ever want an after-school or summer job, or if you want to compete for a spot in a sports camp, an academic summer program, and, eventually, for the all-important college and scholarship applications—you'll need a resume.

In this section, you'll find sample resumes. The main categories featured in this resume are:

- *work, volunteer, and summer experiences*
- *extracurricular activities—school, athletics, community service*
- *awards*

These are the main areas that colleges look at in their best applicants. Remember, colleges are looking for well-balanced, total package kids. It's not all about grades anymore.

TOTAL-PACKAGE KIDS

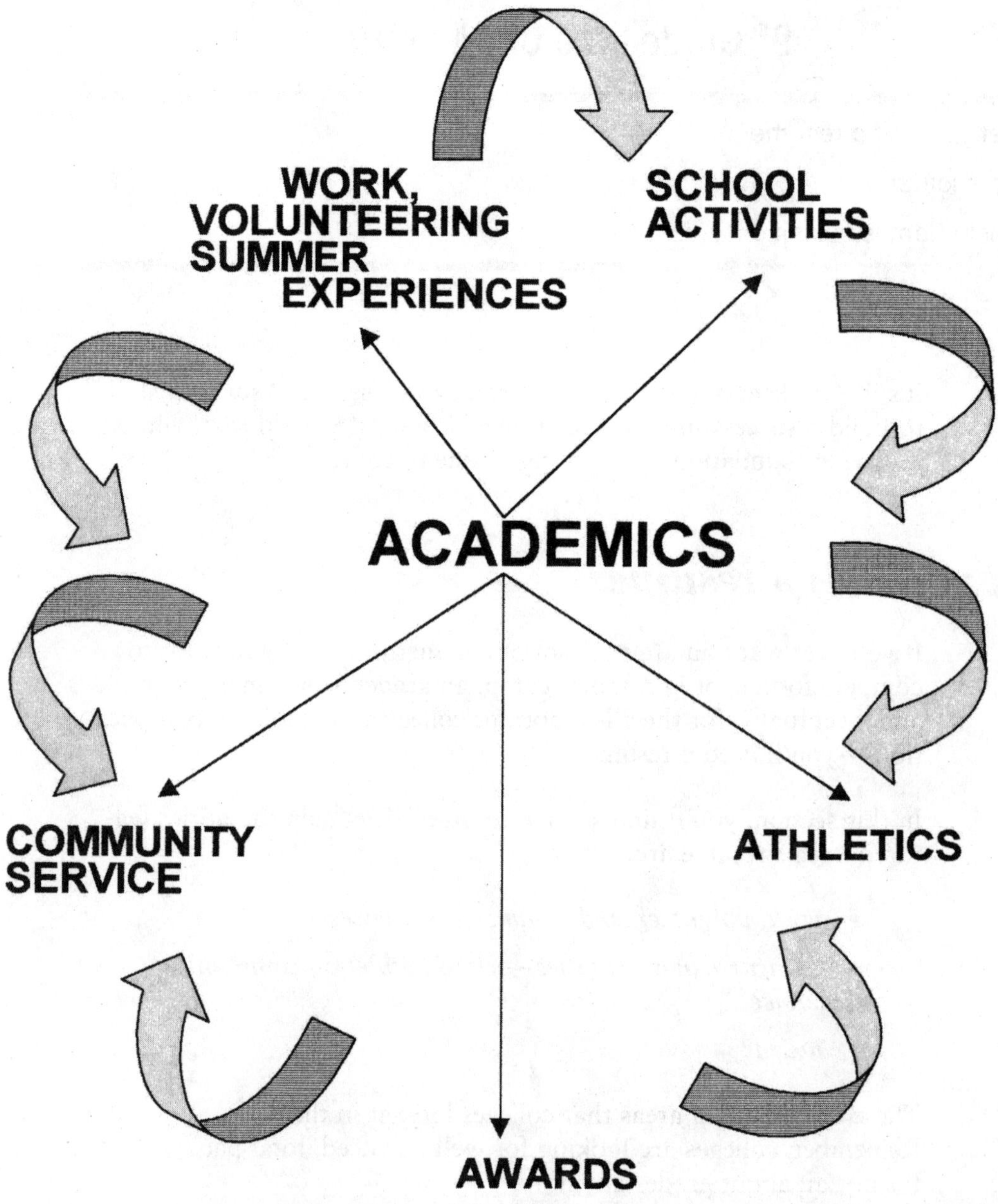

SAMPLE STUDENT RESUME

UNIVERSITY NAME ______________________________

APPLICATION FOR ADMISSION TO THE CLASS OF ______________

Student Name ______________________________

Social Security Number ______________________

EMPLOYMENT, VOLUNTEER WORK, OR SUMMER STUDY EXPERIENCE

Grade(s)	Activity	Hours per wk
10 11 12	Record store associate	25 hrs/week summer 8 hrs/week school yr.
10 11 12	Nursing home volunteer	5 hrs/week summer
9 10 11 12	Museum drawing course	3 hrs/week summer

EXTRACURRICULAR ACTIVITIES

A. SCHOOL

Grade(s)	Activity	Hours per wk
9 10 11 12	Equestrian Club	2 hrs/week
9 10 11 12	Yearbook	2 hrs/week
9 10 11 12	French Club	1 hr/week

B. INTERSCHOLASTIC ATHLETICS

Grade(s)	Activity	Hours Per Wk
9 10 11 12	Basketball	15–20 hrs/week per season

C. COMMUNITY SERVICE

Grade(s)	Activity	Hours Per Wk
11 12	Big Sister	3 hrs/week
10 11 12	Tutor	2 hrs/week

AWARDS

Grade(s)	Activity
9 10 11 12	Honor Roll
9 12	Scholar Athlete Award

STUDENT RESUME WORKSHEET

UNIVERSITY NAME ______________________________

APPLICATION FOR ADMISSION TO THE CLASS OF ______________

Student Name ______________________________

Social Security Number ____________________

LIST ANY EMPLOYMENT, VOLUNTEER WORK, OR SUMMER STUDY EXPERIENCE

Grade(s)	Activity	Hours per wk

EXTRACURRICULAR ACTIVITIES

A. SCHOOL

Grade(s)	Activity	Hours per wk

B. INTERSCHOLASTIC ATHLETICS

Grade(s)	Activity	Hours Per Wk

C. COMMUNITY SERVICE

Grade(s)	Activity	Hours Per Wk

AWARDS

Grade(s)	Activity

As a 9th grader, you're probably staring at a blank sheet. How do you fill it in? Use the sample in this chapter as a framework to help guide you in building your "high school career". Have you always been heavily involved in sports but not very much in after-school activities? Well, here's your chance to balance the picture. It's a good way of being able to step back and look at what areas you need to strengthen.

Don't wait to begin putting together your resume. Resumes will provide invaluable background information to the teachers whom you will ask to write recommendations for you in a few short years. In addition, you can use your resume to help build rich essays for your college and scholarship applications. Make sure to update your resume continually.

When looking at the sample resume, notice in the right-hand column, that there's a time estimate for each activity. Colleges are starting to ask for how much time students spend in activities to filter out the kids who join too many activities in order to pack their resumes. Colleges want to see well-rounded kids who are committed to the activities they are involved in. The name of the game here is **quality,** not quantity.

If you have access to a computer and can keep your resume there, this will be invaluable to you. Applications may not ask for a resume by name, but they will ask for this information in their own format. It is so much easier to be able just to move items around and reformat the information. Then all you have to do is print it out and staple it to the application.

If you are planning to major in the performing or visual arts, you will need to also keep copies of playbills, programs, and so on, to submit with your application or audition to those specialized programs.

Be a joiner

Colleges are looking for well-rounded total-package kids. Besides academics, they are looking for *extracurricular activities.*

It's very tempting and easy to become over-extended with activities. A college admissions officer is not easily fooled. All they have to see is that most of your activities were begun in senior year. Won't it also compensate for bad grades? *Nothing* will hide bad grades. Colleges don't like extremes. Some clubs and sports and good grades are music to their ears. The question is, do you know the tune?

Using your goal-setting tactics, think of your interests and how you want to develop them through school clubs and activities, or work in the community.

- *What skills and interests do you want to explore and perhaps develop?*
- *Are you interested or passionate enough to become a leader in a particular organization?*
- *Are you better suited to be a general member working on projects and events?*

You need to be prepared, either through the interview or resume process, to explain not only what you do, but, also, the reasons why you participate in a certain activity. What makes it special for you, and what do you give back to others through the activity? Has your involvement changed you in any way and how? Keep these in mind as you make choices in your high school life.

Sports fall into the extracurricular activities category. Interscholastic sports can mean playing a sport in a recreational league or acting as record keeper or manager for a team of any kind. These are all considered participating in a sport.

Working during the school year is another form of extracurricular activity, but one that you need to participate in very judiciously. If you can handle your academic life, your extracurricular life, and a job, it will send the message that you have taken initiative, are motivated, well-organized, and mature.

If an after-school job is keeping you from taking a more difficult academic schedule or keeping you from participating in other extracurricular activities, then maybe it's time to reconsider. Save it for the summer when you can devote a lot more time to making some money. This is, of course, assuming your job isn't necessary for you or your family. If it is, make school and your job the priorities, and if you have some extra time, then add a club or sport.

Uncle Sam is calling

Attending a military academy can mean a free college education. An appointment to one of the military service academies can provide you with an excellent education at a highly selective university. But, you must then commit to a contracted number of years of military service as an officer after graduation.

The Service Academies are:

- *United States Military Academy*
- *United States Naval Academy*
- *US Air Force Academy*
- *US Coast Guard Academy*
- *US Merchant Marine Academy*

Besides the normal requirements for a high school graduate, the academies are seeking candidates who have or are:

- *Physically capable of meeting the demands of military training*
- *High desire to serve their country*
- *Highly competitive and motivated*

- *Have exhibited outstanding academic capabilities, with special consideration given to students with honors and accepted Advanced Placement course work*
- *Have exhibited outstanding leadership capabilities*
- *Have exhibited outstanding extracurricular involvement*
- *Have exhibited outstanding sports involvement and leadership*
- *Must be able to accept discipline*
- *Must be flexible, dedicated, and resilient*

If you are considering pursuing an appointment to a military academy, with the exception of the US Coast Guard Academy, you need to start the process during 9th grade. [The US Coast Guard Academy does use the nomination process, but generally follows the remainder of the information listed in this section.] You need to make yourself known, in person, and on paper to your US senators and US Congressional representatives. The vice president of the United States may also make nominations. You can be appointed by any of these. After all nominations have been reviewed and candidates accept their appointments, if there are still available spaces at the academy, then other candidates will be offered appointments.

If possible, it is beneficial, but not necessary, to make an appointment to meet your senators and Congressional representative in person. Also, try to meet them when they make public appearances in your area. These meetings need to happen in 9th grade if possible. Send your senators and representatives cover letters outlining your wishes regarding the military academies along with your resume. Keep them updated of additions to your resume along with recommendations from your teachers or community leaders. (Don't do this more than once or twice a year.) Make a formal request for a nomination during your junior year. Each office has its own procedures, so call and verify them before proceeding.

Other types of nominations (which require additional paperwork) are for children of career military personnel (through presidential appointment), children of deceased or disabled veterans, children of

Medal of Honor recipients, and attendees/members of honor military schools and ROTC (high school and college).

Your college search for the service academies proceeds along much the same lines as any other college search, with the exception of stringent health and physical fitness screenings that are required for academy applicants. At the time of admission, you must be a United States citizen, at least 17 years old, unmarried, have no dependents, and not be pregnant.

You need to make direct contact with the service academy you are interested in during your junior year. At that time, with the submission of a pre-candidate questionnaire, the academy will open a file on you as a pre-candidate. If you pass the initial screening, you will then become a candidate. You will be required to take an extensive qualifying medical exam, a physical aptitude exam, and to be interviewed by an academy information officer. The academies generally have rolling admissions beginning in the fall of senior year, with most of the announcements made in April of senior year.

Military preparatory school

Another avenue of admission to the service academies is to attend a military academy preparatory school for a specified time (usually, less than a year) after high school. These schools help prepare candidates who meet the basic stringent requirements for admission to one of the academies, but need additional preparation in the areas of academics, leadership, and/or physical skills. There is no direct application to these schools. The academies' admissions officers refer promising and highly motivated applicants to the academies to their respective preparatory school.

It can't wait until later. The time is right now. The service academies are considered to be in the "most selective/competitive" category of universities. The characteristics and requirements required of the service academies cannot be met in a year. The latest you can start is in 9th grade. So, if the academies and military service are in your plans, you need to start now to prepare yourself mentally and physically for the road ahead. See the following form "Sample Student Resume" for an example of an academy appointee.

SAMPLE STUDENT RESUME

MILITARY ACADEMY APPOINTEE

UNIVERSITY NAME ____________________

APPLICATION FOR ADMISSION TO THE CLASS OF ____________

Student Name ____________________

Social Security Number ________________

LIST ANY EMPLOYMENT, VOLUNTEER WORK, OR SUMMER STUDY EXPERIENCE

Grade(s)	Activity	Hours per wk
11 12	Science tutor for elementary student	1 hour/week
10–11, 11–12	Football camp	2 weeks/ summer
8–9, 9–10	Baseball camp	2 weeks/ summer

EXTRACURRICULAR ACTIVITIES

A. SCHOOL

Grade(s)	Activity	Hours per wk
12	Spanish Club	1 hour/week
9 10 11 12	Excellence in Mathematics contest	event
10 11 12	Mu Alpha Theta, math honors society Vice President, 11th grade	2 hours/week

9 10 11 12	Student Council President, 12th grade	4 hours/week

B. INTERSCHOLASTIC ATHLETICS

Grade(s)	Activity	Hours Per Wk
11 12	High School Varsity Football captain, 12th grade	15 hours/week
11 12	High School Varsity Baseball captain, 11th grade	15 hours/week
9 10	High School JV Football	15 hours/week
9 10	High School JV Baseball	15 hours/week
	Team captain, 10th grade	

C. COMMUNITY SERVICE

Grade(s)	Activity	Hours Per Wk
12	Special Olympics Steering Committee	2.5 hrs/month
11 12	Teachers aide	20 hrs/summer
9 10 11 12	Boy Scouts	3 hours/week
9 10 11 12	Local Greenpeace chapter	2 hours/week

AWARDS

Grade(s)	Activity
12	Board of Education Award School District in recognition for National Merit Finalist.

12	National Merit Society, Finalist
11 12	National Honor Society, High School Chapter
11 12	Mu Alpha Theta, Mathematics Honors Society
9 10 11 12	High School Honor Roll
9 10 11 12	Scholar Athlete, Gold level, 2 sports
11 12	Regional Chemistry Contest, 8th Place & 9th Place
11 12	Advanced Placement Scholar with Distinction
12	Regional Champions - Football
11	State Champions - Baseball

STUDENT RESUME WORKSHEET

MILITARY ACADEMY APPOINTEE

UNIVERSITY NAME ______________________________

APPLICATION FOR ADMISSION TO THE CLASS OF ______________

Student Name ______________________________

Social Security Number ____________________

LIST ANY EMPLOYMENT, VOLUNTEER WORK, OR SUMMER STUDY EXPERIENCE

Grade(s)	Activity	Hours per wk

EXTRACURRICULAR ACTIVITIES

A. SCHOOL

Grade(s)	Activity	Hours per wk

B. INTERSCHOLASTIC ATHLETICS

Grade(s)	Activity	Hours Per Wk

C. COMMUNITY SERVICE

Grade(s)	Activity	Hours Per Wk

AWARDS

Grade(s)	Activity

SAMPLE STUDENT RESUME #B

UNIVERSITY NAME ______________________________

APPLICATION FOR ADMISSION TO THE CLASS OF ______________

Student Name ______________________________

Social Security Number ______________________

LIST ANY EMPLOYMENT, VOLUNTEER WORK, OR SUMMER STUDY EXPERIENCE

Grade(s)	Activity	Hours per wk
10 11 12	Grocery store bagger Grocery store clerk	25 hrs/week summer 8 hrs/week school yr.
10 11 12	Fast food worker	15 hrs/week summer
9 10 11 12	Nursing home	3 hrs/week summer

EXTRACURRICULAR ACTIVITIES

A. SCHOOL

Grade(s)	Activity	Hours per wk
9 10 11 12	High School choir	continuous
9 10 11 12	Tai Kwon Do	2 hrs/week
9 10 11 12	D.A.R.E.	1hrs/week

B. INTERSCHOLASTIC ATHLETICS

Grade(s)	Activity	Hours Per Wk
9	Stats manager JV baseball	11 hrs/week during season

C. COMMUNITY SERVICE

Grade(s)	Activity	Hours Per Wk
9 10 11 12	Congregation Youth Group	1–1 1/2 hrs/week
9 10 11 12	Boy Scouts	2 hrs/week

AWARDS

Grade(s)	Activity
9	Most Important in Grades—Freshman Class
12	Boy Scout Award
12	Boy Scout Award from congregation

SAMPLE STUDENT RESUME #C

UNIVERSITY NAME ______________________________

APPLICATION FOR ADMISSION TO THE CLASS OF ______________

Student Name ______________________________

Social Security Number ______________________

LIST ANY EMPLOYMENT, VOLUNTEER WORK, OR SUMMER STUDY EXPERIENCE

Grade(s)	Activity	Hours per wk
9 10 11 12	Fast food worker	25 hrs/wk summer 8 hrs/wk school yr.
9 10 11 12	Hospital transportation volunteer	3 hrs/wk summer

EXTRACURRICULAR ACTIVITIES

A. SCHOOL

Grade(s)	Activity	Hours per wk
10 11 12	High School choir Bass soloist, 11th & 12th grades	continuous
9 10 11 12	High School musical productions	-10 hrs/wk during prep & play
10 11 12	Future Teachers Association Treasurer, 12th Grade	2 hrs/week

10 11 12	D.A.R.E. Student speaker to Elementary Schools	event
12	Cadet teaching at high school	10 hrs/week

B. INTERSCHOLASTIC ATHLETICS

Grade(s)	Activity	Hours Per Wk
11 12	High School Varsity Soccer	11 hrs/week
9 10	High School Jr. Varsity Baseball	11 hrs/week
10	High School Jr. Varsity Soccer	11 hrs/week
9	High School Freshman Soccer	11 hrs/week
9 10 11 12	Select soccer team	11 hrs/week

C. COMMUNITY SERVICE

Grade(s)	Activity	Hours Per Wk
9 10 11 12	Congregation Youth Group	3 hrs/week
10 11 12	Packer at Food Pantry	2 hrs/2 weeks
11 12	Congregation Sunday School teacher	3 hrs/week

AWARDS

Grade(s)	Activity
9 10 11 12	Scholar Athlete Awards, Bronze and Silver levels 2 sports
12	Future Teachers of America, Student of the Year
11 12	Choir Student of the Year

SAMPLE STUDENT RESUME #D

UNIVERSITY NAME ____________________

APPLICATION FOR ADMISSION TO THE CLASS OF ____________

Student Name ____________________

Social Security Number ____________________

LIST ANY EMPLOYMENT, VOLUNTEER WORK, OR SUMMER STUDY EXPERIENCE

Grade(s)	Activity	Hours per wk
11 12	Science tutor for elementary student	1 hour/week
10-11-12	Fast food worker	25 hrs/wk summer 8 hrs/wk school yr.
8–9, 9–10,10–11 (Summers)	University Summer Program	3 weeks/ summer

EXTRACURRICULAR ACTIVITIES

A. SCHOOL

Grade(s)	Activity	Hours per wk
10 11 12	High School Orchestra	continuous
12	High School International Club	1 hour/week
10 11 12	High School Drama Club	1 hhour/week
9 10 11 12	High School drama productions back stage crew and props	8–10 hrs/wk during prep & play
11	D.A.R.E. Student speaker to Elementary, Schools	event

9 10 11 12	Excellence in Mathematics contest	event

B. INTERSCHOLASTIC ATHLETICS

Grade(s)	Activity	Hours Per Wk
9 10 11 12	Congregation Soccer, recreational league	4 hours/week
10	High School Jr. Varsity Soccer.	11 hrs/week
9	High School Freshman Girls Soccer.	11 hrs/week

C. COMMUNITY SERVICE

Grade(s)	Activity	Hours Per Wk
12	Congregation Youth Group Representative to Congregation Council	2.5 hrs/month
11 12	High School Spring (Special) Olympics Committee	2 hours/week
9 10 11 12	Congregation Youth Group	3 hours/week
10 11 12	Congregation Youth Group Core Team	1 hour/week
9 10	Congregation Vacation School Teachers aide	20 hours/ summer

AWARDS

Grade(s)	Activity
12	Board of Educastion Award School District. in recognition for National Merit Finalist.
12	National Merit Society, Finalist
11 12	National Honor Society, High School Chapter
11	Mu Alpha Theta, Mathematics Honors Society
9 10 11 12	High School Honor Roll

Other military-based college programs

ROTC Scholarships

The Reserve Officer Training Corp (ROTC) Scholarship is a program that offers a certain amount of funds to be used toward tuition at an ROTC participating college. You will also receive a small living stipend. The Army also adds funds for books and supplies. However, you have to go through the regular admissions process for the school you pick.

Regular ROTC program

Candidates join the program during their first year and work within the program for no compensation until their junior and senior years. At that time, they will be paid a small stipend

THE INTERNET

Websites for the U.S. Military

Military options website

http://www.myfuture.com

Each of the academies have their own websites that encompass vast amounts of information. Contact the admissions department officers by e-mail and download the pre-candidate questionnaires.

United States Military Academy at West Point, NY

http://www.usma.edu

United States Naval Academy at Annapolis, MD

http://www.nadn.navy.mil

US Air Force Academy at Colorado Springs, CO

http://www.usafa.af.mil/

US Coast Guard Academy at New London, CT

http://www.cga.edu

US Merchant Marine Academy at Kings Point, NY

http://www.usmma.edu

Highlights

★ Get yourself a resume. This will help you when you are applying for summer programs, jobs, even when you are filling out college applications. It will be your own checklist of your student career, which will help you figure out what you may need to cut back on and add more of.

★ Be a joiner. In case it hasn't been emphasized enough yet, colleges want well-rounded individuals. They want to see that you can juggle a few things and do them well. But beware of getting in over your head, go for the three or four clubs, sports, volunteer groups, that truly interest you.

★ If Uncle Sam calls, you'd better answer. If you are thinking of pursuing a military career and education, start the process now. It is a very detailed and time-consuming path and must start in 9th grade.

Chapter 4

10th Grade—The Clock Is Ticking

- ✔ Pick a college, any college
- ✔ collegesearch.com
- ✔ Decisions, decisions...
- ✔ PSAT...already?
- ✔ To AP/IB or not to AP/IB

Pick a college, any college

Universities, community colleges, public, private. The array of choices available is confusing. What are the differences? The similarities? Better yet, which college will accept you? Here's a quick rundown of the different colleges available to you.

Universities usually consist of a handful of colleges such as the College of Arts and Sciences. Universities also have a graduate school that offers advanced degrees. What makes a university different from a college is that it has a graduate school.

Community colleges award students associate degrees once they complete a two-year program.

College without the stomachaches. This is a phrase many students use when referring to community colleges. If you are not ready to enter into a four-year commitment, this type of college can be a better option. In addition, if your grades are not good enough to get you into the 4-year college of your choice, this could be the ideal alternative for you. If you're an athlete who needs to improve your stats, community college could be a great choice.

Then there are the engineering schools such as MIT and Georgia Tech. They teach applied science which is used for everything building bridges and cars to making the hardware that you use to log-on to the Internet.

Notre Dame (Catholic) and Brigham Young (Mormon) are two religious-affiliated colleges. In these colleges, their religious denomination plays a major role in campus life. However, students of all faiths (or no faiths) are welcome.

In addition to the different types of "higher education" choices, there's the matter of public schools versus private schools. There is a great deal of difference in their respective costs.

(These figures reflect total costs—tuition, room and board, etc.)

Public	Private
Usually $8,000 or more	Usually $20,000 or more
Subsidized by the state	Funded by tuition, alumni donations, and other endowments
Harder to get into if you don't live in that state	usually more financial aid offered

Smith and Wellesley are two single-sex colleges. These private colleges are a good option for women who are more comfortable in a female-only environment. So that we don't leave men out, one option for them is Hobart, which happens to be the brother school of Smith.

Now that we've gone over the different types of schools available to you, we must consider how pick from the 3,500 colleges and universities available. From directories to on-line resources, even to face-to-face encounters, there is a wealth of information available that's just waiting for you.

The most traditional source of college information can be found in your local bookstore (as well as some libraries.) The next time you go into a bookstore, visit the college reference section. You'll find comprehensive college directories that list everything from college size, admission requirements, to the different majors available. Two well-known college directories are: *Complete Book of Colleges* by Princeton Review, and *Peterson's College & University Almanac, 1999.*

In addition to traditional directories, a more effective tool in your college search process is right at your fingertips. This is the Internet.

collegesearch.com

Only a few short years ago, the words, "Internet" and "World Wide Web", had no meaning except for a few scientists trading information around the world. Today, everyone is on the Web. Most colleges now have their own websites which feature everything from information that's listed in the college catalogs to virtual tours that place you right in the middle of their campus.The information featured on college websites is that is probably more current and up-to-date than a catalog that may only be published once every two years. Check the "date updated on" noted at the bottom of the screen to verify the age of the Web page.

How do you start searching the Internet?

If you have a particular college you want to look up, use a search engine to locate the Web address for that college. Or you can key in the exact address (URL) of the college from a catalog you may have received in the mail or from your guidance counselor.

Use one of the following main search engines to find a college that you're looking for:

Alta Vista	http://altavista.digital.com also at http://www.altavista.com
Excite	http://www.excite.com
Infoseek	http://guide.infoseek.com
LookSmart	http://looksmart.com
Lycos	http://lycos.cs.cmu.edu also at http://www.lycos.com
Magellan	http://www.mckinley.com
MetaCrawler	http://www.metacrawler.com
Netscape	http://netscape.com
Search.com	http://search.com
Snap	http://www.snap.com
Web Crawler	http://www.webcrawler.com
Yahoo	http://www.yahoo.com

What if you don't know which college you want to get information on? One of the first sites you can go to is "Selecting a School: A Guided Tour" (http://www.adventuresineducation.org/selecting). This site lists points that you should keep in mind when selecting a college. After you have come up with a list of criteria, log onto one of the larger sites that will help you make specific choices. These sites will help you sort and filter schools and link you up with their websites. These sites include:

American School Counselors Association

http://www.schoolcounselor.org

Think College, US Department of Education

http://www.ed.gov/

CollegeNet

http://www.collegenet.com

Crash Course in College Admission By the National Association for College Admission Counselors

http://www.nacac.com

CollegeEdge

http://www.collegeedge.com

Princeton Review Best Colleges

http://www.princetonreview.com/

Historically Black Colleges & Universities (HBCO)

http://eric-web.tc.columbia.edu/hbcu/index.html

U.S. Universities and Community Colleges

http://www.utexas.edu/world/univ/

College Board Online

http://www.collegeboard.org/

Princeton Review College Homepage

http://www.review.com/undergrad/college_homepage.html

Peterson's

http://www.petersons.com

Internet Public Library

http://ipl.org/teen

College View Search

http://www.collegeview.com

College Zone

http://www.kaplan.com

Minority On-Line Information Systems (MOLIS)

http://web.fie.com/web/mol

PARENTS CORNER

If you want to know which colleges rank the highest, long onto one of these sites:

Money Magazine's College Guide

http://www.pathfinder.com/money/

U.S. News & World Report

http://www.usnews.com/usnews/edu/home.htm

What's next?

You've used the Internet to narrow down the colleges that you want to investigate further. You've taken virtual tours of all the campuses. You've printed out information for your files. You've e-mailed the admission departments, e-mailed and chatted with student ambassadors, and maybe even added your name to a few mailing lists and subscribed to relevant newsgroups. And you've done all of this without leaving your chair!

Your next step brings you back from virtual to the real world. The Internet and the information on the World Wide Web are only tools. You now need to make phone contact with admissions staff of the colleges that interest you. You need to ask for leads, information, and feedback from your high school counseling staff, your teachers, older friends, and even your parents.

Be very wary when working with information from the Web! Make sure you verify information you have received, just as you do when you get a piece of information in the mail. You have to determine how much of the material on an online site is accurate.

Watch out for fraud, especially in the financial aid/scholarship search areas. These scams abound. Go to the Federal Trade Commission's (FTC) "Project $cholar$cam" for scam warnings:

http://www.ftc.gov/bcp/conline/edcams/scholarship/index.html

Decisions, decisions...

When you are gathering information on specific colleges, begin making a comparison list. This list should feature everything from how many students attend the college to where the college is located. These factors will be extremely important to you when you have to make your final decision. Here's a sampling:

PleaseAcceptMe U

Distance	West Coast? East Cost? North? South? Overseas? Midwest? How far away do you want to be from home? From your friends? A driveway? A 6-hour flight away?
Size of Campus	University of Michigan? or College of 100 Students? Do you just want to be another number? Or are you looking for the personal touch—a family atmosphere?

City vs. Suburb	Bright Lights, Big City? or, Anytown USA? Do you need to be near sky-scrapers and all-night delis? Or, are you looking for trees, malls, and quickie-marts? Think not only about the size and type of your campus, but also the campus surroundings.
Types of Majors	There's nothing wrong if you don't know yet what you want to major in. (Let's face it, some college juniors still don't know.) However, if you know that you want to become—say a veterinarian—then it makes sense now for you to pick a school that offers this type major.
Residence	Dorm? Frat House? Off-Campus Apt? Mom and Dad? What kind of housing do you want to live in? Whom do you want to live with (by yourself, your best-friend, people of the same ethnic background, same-sex dorms?).
Your Chances of Getting In	More about this will be discussed later in the book. For now, you should begin comparing ballpark tuition costs (remember, private schools are nearly three times more expensive than public schools
Cost	Okay, up to this point, it's been all about you (what you're looking for in the college). Now the tables are turned. Do the colleges want you? They will be looking at your high school grades, your college

entrance test scores, and a host of other criteria (including GPA, ranking, extracurricular, and more.) You need to eliminate those schools that, realistically, right now, would be too competitive for you.

You'll see that once you begin creating this list of comparisons, eliminating colleges will be quite easy. If you don't like to live in a rural or be too far away to visit your parents every weekend, you can immediately cross many schools off your list.

TIME OUT

When deciding whether or not a college is too competitive for you, also think about those schools that would be too easy for you. That is, they are not challenging enough for you. You may be offered a full 4- year scholarship at a local college, but would you really get something out of your experience?

PARENTS CORNER

Parents, you can help your child get more college information by making appointments with him/her to talk with guidance counselors, colleagues, and mutual friends who've attended college. Word of mouth can be as valuable as the written word.

PSAT... already?

Yes. And not just the PSAT, but the SAT, PLAN, ACT, CLEP, and TOEFL.

The Preliminary Scholastic Assessment Test (PSAT) is the preparatory test for the **Scholastic Assessment Test (SAT)** also known as the SAT I.

The PSAT, when taken in junior year, is required for National Merit and National Achievement Recognition and Scholarship applicants. You should take this test for practice in your sophomore year and for real in your junior year for entry into the National Merit Scholarship Corporation programs.

Both the PSAT and the SAT have two sections: Verbal and Mathematics. The PSAT is used as a gauge to see how you'll do on the SAT. The highest possible scores on the SAT are 800 on each section. It is a good idea to take the SAT more than once—the first time during junior year, if not before. The SAT is the test of choice by colleges on either coast. It is necessary to take it.

If you are taking college level course work during high school, it's a good idea to take the SAT II achievement tests for those subjects at the end of the school year. If you wait until senior year, you most likely won't remember as much as if you had taken it that same year.

The PSAT and SAT I and II are sponsored by the College Board.

The **PLAN** is a preliminary form of the **American College Testing (ACT)** and is constructed similarly to the ACT. It is a one-hour test that is offered at your school sometime between October and December. Check with your guidance office in September to verify dates and to get a registration form. Taking the PLAN is especially important if you plan to take the ACT.

The ACT has several parts based on curriculum areas: English, Math, Social Science, Reading Skills and Scientific Reasoning. The highest possible composite score is a 36. This test is very popular in the Midwest, and is gaining acceptance with colleges on either coast. It is a good idea to take the ACT more than once—the first time during junior year—if not before.

Most likely you don't know which schools you will be applying to until late in your junior year or at the beginning of your senior year. Therefore, since you might not know for sure what tests will be required for admission, plan on taking both the ACT and SAT.

The **College Level Examination Program** (CLEP) is also a product of the College Board. This series of subject tests allows students to gain college credit for knowledge they have gained through life experiences and/or their own independent study. These are given throughout the year and are often available through your college guidance counseling office. You will need to take these before you schedule courses.

The **Test of English as a Foreign Language** (TOEFL) is required if English is not your native language. You will need to take the TOEFL in addition to the SAT and/or ACT.

Test dates and registration deadlines for each test are listed in the following form and on the tear-out card. Check with your guidance counseling office or the test's website for verification of dates and the fee for each test.

Make copies of completed registration forms and the check. Keep a separate file for each test.

PSAT test dates

Tuesday, October 12, 1999
Saturday, October 16, 1999
Verify with your guidance counseling office or
Website: http://www.collegeboard.org/html/testdates001.html

SAT I and II Program Tests

Preliminary 1999-2000 Test Dates

National Test Dates	Test	Registration Deadlines U.S.	U.S. Late
10/9/1999	SAT I and SAT II	9/14/1999	9/18/1999
11/6/1999	SAT I, SAT II and Language Tests with Listening	10/1/1999	10/13/1999
12/4/1999	SAT I and SAT II	10/29/1999	11/10/1999
1/22/2000	SAT I and SAT II	12/17/1999	12/30/1999
4/8/2000	SAT I only	3/3/2000	3/15/2000
5/6/2000	SAT I and SAT II	3/31/2000	4/12/2000
6/3/2000	SAT I and SAT II	4/28/2000	5/10/2000

Sunday administrations will occur the day after each Saturday administration listed above.
Verify with your guidance counseling office or
Website: http://www.collegeboard.org/html/testdates001.html

CLEP test dates

Tests may be given any day of the month selected by the test center. The English Composition with Essay Examination will be given nationally only in January, April, June and October.
Verify with your guidance counseling office or
Website: http://www.collegeboard.org/html/testdates001.html

ACT ASSESSMENT TEST DATES

1999-2000

Test Date	Regular Registration	Late Registration
September 25, 1999 (available only in Arizona, California, Florida, Georgia, Illinois, Indiana, Maryland, Nevada, North Carolina, Pennsylvania, South Carolina, Texas and Washington	August 20, 1999	September 3, 1999
October 23, 1999	September 17, 1999	October 1, 1999
December 11, 1999	November 5, 1999	November 19, 1999
February 12, 2000 (not available in New York)	January 7, 2000	January 21, 2000
April 1, 2000	February 25, 2000	March 10, 2000
June 10, 2000	May 5, 2000	May 19, 2000

Verify with your guidance counseling office or Website:
http://www.act.org/app/REGIST/ACT dates. html

You'll like the sound of this. Certain types of calculators are allowed for use in these tests. ALWAYS consult the registration guide for each test for particular calculator details as they change from year-to-year. You don't want to show up on the day of the exam with the wrong calculator.

Don't be upset if you don't test well. Keep in mind that the test score is only one of several components in the college admission game. It is not the only thing colleges look at. Consider test study sessions given either in classes or by home study. There are study materials, computer programs, and video-based learning materials available for preparing for these tests. Often, they are available in your high school guidance office.

Sunday test dates are available at some sites for those students who have religious or other restrictions for Saturday mornings.

For more information on the PSAT, SAT I and II, the Advanced Placement program, CLEP and TOEFL exams, consult the College Board's website at

http://www.collegeboard.org

The College Board offers a wealth of current information along with being a source of test and course preparation materials, including sample questions, sections of tests, and test taking tips. The College Board also sells test prep software.

The Educational Testing Service administers all the testing for the College Board. ETS's website also has mini online tests to practice on and test prep software for sale.

http://www.ets.org

For information on the ACT and its test preparation consult their website at

http://www.act.org

The Princeton Review's website also offers test preparation advice and services at

http://www.princetonreview.com

Stanford Testing Systems offers a free online service as well as software for sale at

http://www.testprep.com

GoCollege's website offers different versions of the SAT and ACT online for you to practice on at

http://www.gocollege.com

Kaplan's website offers their test prep software for sale at

http://www1.kaplan.com

The Learning Company offers testprep software for sale at

http://www.learningco.com

For the exam, be sure to:

- *Eat a nutritious dinner on Friday night.*
- *Get a good night's sleep.*
- *Get up early enough to be truly awake by the time of the test.*
- *Eat a nutritious breakfast on Saturday morning.*

Once you have taken the test, you have 6-8 weeks before your score comes back.

If you have certified special physical and/or learning and/or Attention Deficit Disorder (ADD) disabilities, special test conditions, and/or suspension of test-taking time limitations may be arranged. You need to mark the disability on the registration form, talk to your high school guidance counselor, and talk to the test administrator the morning of the test. Refer to the test registration packet of each test for specific instructions and waivers. These disabilities will also be noted on the test result form that is sent to the universities.

To AP/IB or not to AP/IB

In Chapter 1, you learned that colleges want kids who take risks. How much risk should you take? The answer is based on your own academic history and how hard you want to work. If you have a strong academic background, you might consider taking college level course work while you attend high school.

The Advanced Placement (AP) program is a product of the College Entrance Examination Board. Most high schools offering college level work offer it through the AP program. The AP program is widely accepted by the majority of colleges in the United States. There are specialized courses for teachers designed to support teaching this high level and stringent course work.

The program is a series of core curricular tests given at the end of each school year for each class you have taken based on the specialized curriculum outlined by the College Entrance Examination Board. Over your high school career, you may take any number of AP courses and exams. You can take the course without taking the exam, though taking the exam is recommended if you have done well in the course. If you are motivated to that level of independent study, you can take an AP exam without taking an AP course. If your score on an AP exam meets the scoring requirements of the college you ultimately attend, you will be granted college credit based on that exam. Different colleges grant differing college credit for each AP exam.

The International Baccalaureate (IB) program is a comprehensive and challenging honors program—the Diploma Program—covering the last two years of high school. The IB program is an international high school program offered at 800 schools in nearly 100 countries around the world. It is offered at over 250 high schools in the United States. IB's college-level curriculum is based on a global interpretation of academic subject areas. Since this curriculum is internationally based, participating students must work with their high school guidance counselor to ensure they meet their high school graduation requirements. You have to attend an IB member high school to participate in the IB program. A high school has to apply to the International Baccalaureate Organization and follow the entire process to gain authorization to be an IB member school. If your IB scores meet the scoring requirements of the college you ultimately attend, you will be granted college credit based on that exam.

Along with a rigorous pre-university traditional liberal arts curriculum, IB has some unique components:

- *The Theory of Knowledge (TOK) seeks to develop a coherent approach to learning that transcends and unifies the academic subjects and encourages appreciation of other cultural perspectives.*
- *The Creativity Action, Service (CAS) requirement takes seriously the importance of life outside the world of the classroom and studying. It provides a counterbalance to a heavy academic load. CAS's goal is educating the whole person and fostering a more compassionate citizen.*
- *Diploma candidates are required to undertake research and write an extended essay of at least 4,000 words. The essay component requires independent research and writing skills.*

The curriculum consists of six areas surrounding the three special components. The six areas are Language (1st language), Second Language, Individuals and Societies (social studies), Experimental Sciences, Mathematics, and Arts & Electives.

Individual subject tests are scored 1 through 7. A diploma is awarded if there is a total of 24 awarded points plus satisfactory completion of the TOK and CAS. Students who take less than the full program will receive certificates of examination. Thirty thousand students participate each year in IB and 80% of the diploma candidates succeeded in earning their diplomas.

Some school districts also offer the Middle Years Program that corresponds to the United States' grades 6 through 10. The Middle Years Program is not required for students to attain the IB diploma program. An incredibly strong academic background is advised for those wanting to earn an IB diploma who do not have access to the Middle Years Program.

THE INTERNET

Information on the Advanced Placement program, testing and current test dates may be found on the College Board's website at

http://www.collegeboard.org

The Educational Testing Service (ETS) is the organization that administers the Advanced Placement program's testing for the College Board. Their website is

http://www.ets.org

and is also linked to the College Board's website.

Information on the International Baccalaureate Program may be found at their Web site at

http://www.ibo.org

Joint cooperative course programs between high schools and a local university is another way to obtain college credit in high school. High school teachers teach these courses, but the university governs the final exams. The grade scored on the exam given at the high school will be the grade given on the transcript from that college for the student. During the time the student is enrolled in these courses, the student is also officially enrolled at that college. These courses are sometimes referred to as 1-8-1-8 courses.

Dual or shared enrollment is another format for gaining college credit. This is when you attend classes at both high school and a local college. This often occurs when a student is more academically advanced than the courses available at his/her high school in a curricular area. Dual enrollment requires a degree of cooperation between the student high school guidance counselor and the college. Timing and logistical problems have to be analyzed to make dual enrollment possible. Just be sure you can handle this. Also keep in mind that you'll be missing a major part of the social life at your high school.

Independent Study is another form of acquiring advanced course work while in high school. You submit a proposal outlining the scope, objectives, timetable, and assessment of the independent study investigation. Then you need to find a teacher who is willing to be your sponsor for this project. Independent study options can also involve a college professor or a professional acting as a mentor to the student. This course-work has to be finished within one academic year, unless other arrangements have been made. Independent study is one of the most difficult options open to a high school student. This option requires you to be able to work and study independently of a classroom environment. You will require immense discipline, time management, and study skills.

Correspondence courses available through universities are yet another way to obtain college credit while in high school. This option requires you to be able to work and study independently of a classroom environment and teacher. Often there is no interaction with a human being for these courses except a proctor at exam time. You will be given textbook materials and assignments. The assignments are then turned in either by mail or by e-mail (depending upon the option of the university). The corrected answer sheet is returned along with the next assignment. You are given a set amount of time to finish the course work and take the exams, but you can petition to extend the time if necessary.

PARENTS CORNER

Advanced Placement/International Baccalaureate (AP/IB) courses are by definition difficult and time-intensive curricula. The decision to take AP/IB or dual enrollment not only requires an academic commitment on your child's part, but also from you. Although your child is in high school and at home, he/she is away at college. Be there for your child as much as you can to make the year that much more manageable.

What good comes out of all this extra work?

- *If you choose to participate, it challenges you to excel. It shows colleges you are willing to take high degrees of academic risk.*

- *The course work requires you to become organized and perfect time-management skills to acquire vast amounts of knowledge in a short time period. It also gives you the opportunity to acquire a high degree of critical thinking and writing skills.*
- *If your scores on the nationally scored exams reach a level preset by the university of your choice, you will receive college credit hours for that AP/IB course(s). Any basic first year courses you can get credit for before actually attending a university is a plus.*
- *Even if the college credit hours do nothing at first to benefit you directly in curriculum areas, upon entry to the university, you are rated by hours at a level higher than a first semester freshman.*
- *College credit hours allow the student to have extra time and room in his/her schedule, to qualify for undergraduate research earlier, to study and/or to work abroad, and even to acquire multiple degrees, majors and/or minors.*
- *For a highly selective university, the admissions directors would rather see a "B" or even a "C" in an AP/IB/dual enrollment course, than an "A" in a much easier course.*

These specialized high level curricula in some schools are only available to juniors and seniors. In some schools, talented and well-prepared sophomores and perhaps freshmen are also able to participate in these programs. The keys to the success for any student taking these courses are well-developed study skills and rigorous academic preparation.

College admission officials are looking for well-rounded "total-package" kids. If taking multiple AP/IB/dual enrollment courses prevents you from being involved in extra-curricular activities, community involvement, and/or sports, then maybe cutting back on some of this academic load might be a good idea.

What's the point here? Colleges want to see well-balanced risk takers. SAFE is something they can find anywhere!

If your high school does not have AP/IB, honors or accelerated courses available, consider taking courses at a local college. Show that taking a risk is important to you.

Purchase study guides for each of the AP courses you take. Get them at the beginning of the academic year, not a month before the national exam. There are several well-known publishers of the AP study guides and these can be found at any major bookstore.

Highlights

★ It's time to begin the long, sometimes painful process of choosing a college. But this can be easy. All you need to do for now is to familiarize yourself with what is out there.

★ Get on the Web. Experiment with search engines and figure out where to go for important information.

★ Take the PSAT for practice. The score doesn't matter and will make the next time around—when it counts—a lot easier.

★ Familiarize yourself now with the different tests out there for college. If you are sure you know what schools you'll be applying to, find out now exactly which exams they require. If you aren't sure yet (which is fine, you have plenty of time left), consider taking both the SAT and the ACT.

★ Be a risk-taker. Colleges love them. If you think you can handle the added work, study, and possible stress, take a college level class.

Chapter 5

If Only Money Did Grow on Trees

Paying for College

- ✔ It costs how much?
- ✔ You pay this much
- ✔ FAFSA
- ✔ The profile
- ✔ Free and not so free money
- ✔ Financial aid on the Web
- ✔ Your financial timeline

Paying for college can be difficult. If you're a parent, the word "tuition" can bring on panic attacks, headaches and sleepless nights. If you're a student, it means more forms, calculations, and deadlines to meet. If applying to college weren't enough, now you've got to worry about paying for it, too? Since the cost of college can range anywhere from $15,000 to $30,000 per year, you have to devise a plan as to how you are going to pay for it (unless, of course, money is no object for you). But, the amount of money you actually have to pay is not as high as you think. In this chapter you'll discover the many financial options available to you.

Saving for college

Financing a college education out of current cash flow is almost impossible except for a very few families. In an ideal world, families would be able to save all they would need to send their children to their first choice college. But this is the real world and, most families have not been able to save even a third to a half of the funding needed.

Besides the traditional savings accounts and investment accounts, in recent years, several new avenues have opened up for families trying to prepare financially for the college years. There are educational IRA's which are tax-free when used for college tuition and fees. (These IRA's presently have a $500 per year limitation on annual contributions.) There are US Savings Bonds designed to be tax-free if used for college tuition and fees. (There are family income limitations on who can take advantage of these programs. Please consult your financial/tax professional if you have any questions.)

Over 30 states presently offer some form of college savings plan. As this is written, more states are considering adding these programs as an aid to their residents. You will need to investigate what type of program your state has to offer. Some programs allow you to save for college and use these funds for college anywhere in the United States. Others are restricted to state colleges within your state. Some states restrict the plans only to tuition and fees, while other states allow the savings funds to be used not only for tuition and fees, but also for room and board and other college living expenses. Some plans require installment payments and cancel your plan and charge a penalty if you can't make those payments. With some of the plans, the contribution limits will not allow enough to be saved to cover the cost of college. You need to ask about fees charged to have the account. At this time, this type of savings decreases financial aid awards by the amount in the savings account for that child. All of the state college-savings plans are not tax-free, but tax-deferred, until used for college. Your best bet is to do a lot of research, ask questions and keep current, because these plans constantly change.

If you began saving for college when your children were infants or toddlers, your family has a good chance of being in great shape for the next several years. If you are concerned about how to handle the college funds during these last few years before college, contact your financial planner for possible strategies of balancing investment income growth, safety, and availability.

If you began saving for college when your children were in grade school, your family also has a good chance of being great shape for the next several years. If you are also concerned about how to handle the college funds during these last few years before college, contact your financial planner.

If you began saving for college when your children entered into high school, or circumstances prevented your family from saving in any appreciable manner, do not despair. There are methods for meeting the cost of attending college. Those methods, which will be discussed later in this chapter, include loan programs available for students and parents, grants, scholarships, gifts, and work-study programs.

For all families, the answer lies in doing your research. Ask for professional financial advice and have honest family financial discussions. There may be some sacrifices required by both the teen and parents.

It costs how much?

The newspapers and television news are often full of stories of how much it will cost to go to college. Figures in the press range from $10,000 per year to $30,000 per year. Don't let any of this frighten you away. If a student chooses to go to a two-year community college, the tuition presently averages less than $1,500 per year. For in-state four-year colleges or universities, the tuition is often lower than $5,000 per year. For the vast majority of all colleges in the country, the tuition is under $15,000 per year. Only the most expensive private four-year universities have prices that are over $20,000 per year. Don't be dismayed. Even for the top schools, financial aid is available that may bring your cost in line with what can be afforded.

There is good news on college tuition costs. There is a movement among some colleges, even the top ones, to start containing the annual rise in costs.

When planning how much you will have to pay to attend the school of your dreams, don't just focus on tuition. When figuring out actual costs, you also have to consider the following:

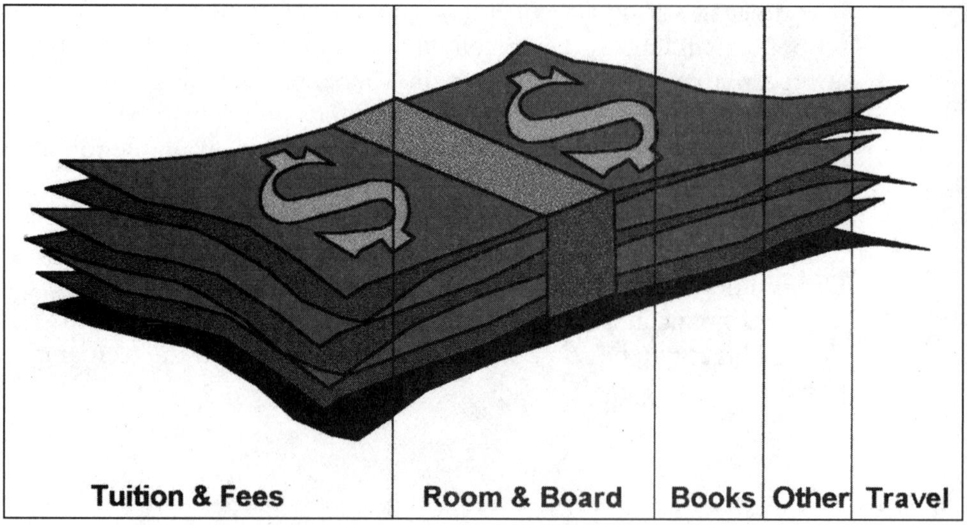

Tuition and fees

These are the cost of your classes and the associated fees such as student activities, library, technology, and health center fees.

Room and board

If you live on campus, room and board is the cost of your dorm room and your meal plan. Most room fees are quoted on the basis of a two-student dorm room, with singles being more, and triple or quads usually costing less. There is usually a variety of meal plans available, ranging from 14 meals, to 21 meals, to 35 meals (usually for athletes) per week. The choices vary from school to school. For those freshmen from out-of-town, most universities require that they live on campus and purchase at least a minimum meal plan.

Books

Books include all the textbooks, lab books, supplies, and materials to attend courses. Some courses require more than others. A literature course is going to require a lot of books. A science lab course is going to require some safety equipment, lab books, and, perhaps, lab fees. A studio art course is going to require art supplies and materials.

Other

Other encompasses personal expenses that are needed to live such as medical insurance, furnishings and bedding for your dorm room, and laundry.

Travel

If you live out-of-town, travel is the cost of getting back and forth from college and for any trips between college and home. If you live in-town and off-campus, this is the cost for getting back and forth to school each day.

You pay this much

Expected Family Contribution (EFC)

Financial need in the college financial aid game is not what you think you and your parents can afford to spend each year for you to go to college. Instead, financial need is computed by a national formula called the EFC. Every student will receive an EFC when he/she applies for financial aid from the government after they file a Free Application for Federal Student Aid (FAFSA). You can get a free copy of a FAFSA at your high school guidance office or you can download one from the U.S. Department of Education website at http://www.ed.gov.

There are several estimators available which will give you an idea of what your family's expected contribution would be. One estimator is available through American College Testing (ACT), the service that also offers the ACT college entrance exam. There is a small fee to use this estimator service. There is also an on-line estimator available on the College Board's website that is free to use. (See the Internet website box for the URL address.) To use these estimators, you will need the basic financial information that you used on your most recent income tax return.

These estimators give two ways of computing your family's EFC. Each depends on whether the student is considered a dependent or an independent student, as defined by the IRS for tax purposes. One way of estimating is by using the federal methodology option. This will give you a general idea of what your EFC is for federal college financial aid programs. The second way of estimating is by using the institutional methodology option. With a few more questions to answer, you will get a rough idea of how much money a private college will give you based on their own terms.

For good financial planning, a family should be looking at the estimators no later than the fall of the teen's junior year in high school and, preferably, during the freshman or sophomore year. This figure will only be an estimate, but it will help you prepare your college financial plan by giving you an idea of what you will be expected to contribute toward your teen's education.

The EFC leads you to the amount of financial aid for which your student is eligible.

Demonstrated financial need

The Demonstrated Financial Need is the amount of financial aid for which your student is eligible. Demonstrated Financial Need may be met by any or a combination of work-study, grants, scholarships, and loans. Seventy percent of all US student aid is supplied by the Student Financial Assistance Programs, which are administered and funded by the federal government.

If there are any special circumstances that might affect your financial ability to pay that will not show up in the questions asked by the financial aid forms, you need to explain the circumstances to the financial aid departments at the schools you are thinking of attending.

Free Application for Federal Student Aid (FAFSA)

The main financial aid computational tool used by colleges is the FAFSA. This form is available from your student's high school guidance counseling office by November of each year. You can also download and print the FAFSA from the Department of Education's website or you can file on-line using the Department of Education's FAFSA express site. (See the Internet website boxes for the URL addresses.)

Senior year

December:	Obtain the FAFSA. Start preparing financial information for the FAFSA. Attend a financial aid workshop, if necessary
January—February:	Complete the FAFSA and send it as soon as Possible after January 1st, but not before.

File the FAFSA as soon after January 1st of senior year as possible. Ideally the family should fill out and mail the FAFSA using estimated tax data. You should then re-file a corrected Student Aid Report as soon as you and your teen's Federal 1040 income tax forms are completed. The reason for this timetable is that often Federal aid dollars are awarded on a first-come first-serve basis.

Filling out the FAFSA requires patience and sometimes a bit of help. However, if you have all of the necessary documents in front of you, then it should only take about 20 minutes to fill out. This information will be for the calendar and tax year that ended December 31st of your teen's senior year. The documents you will need are the following:

Earned income for both you and your family;

Federal tax return from that year;

Information on the value of any business or investments;

Amount of money in savings and checking accounts.

The FAFSA comes with three pages of instructions plus a worksheet. Financial aid departments of your local universities may offer workshops on how to fill out these forms. Usually, they are held each December and/or January. Contact the financial aid departments of your local universities directly for information. Later in this chapter, you will find sample worksheets as well as an actual FAFSA form to show you how manageable the financial aid process can be when you're organized.

After you have completed the FAFSA; send it in and within a few weeks you will receive a Student Aid Report (SAR) that will give you the amount the government believes you should pay next year for college. This figure is the Expected Family Contribution (EFC) and will be forwarded to the colleges you indicated in your FAFSA. The colleges will then use this information to compile their financial aid packages for your teen.

TIME OUT

File the FAFSA as soon after January 1st of senior year as possible. Ideally, you should fill out and mail the FAFSA using estimated tax data. If some of your estimates are inaccurate, you can plug in the up-to-date information on the Student Aid Report and re-file it.

On the following four pages pages is an actual FAFSA. **The FAFSA shown here is for sample purposes only and is not to be used as an actual form to be submitted or used for actual calculation purposes.** The information and calculations change from year-to-year.

Free Application for Federal Student Aid

OMB 1840-0110

July 1, 1999 — June 30, 2000 school year

Step One: For questions 1-37, leave blank any questions that do not apply to you (the student).

1-3. Your name — 1. LAST NAME | 2. FIRST NAME | 3. M.I.

4-7. Your permanent mailing address — 4. NUMBER AND STREET (INCLUDE APARTMENT NUMBER) | 5. CITY (AND COUNTRY, IF NOT U.S.) | 6. STATE | 7. ZIP CODE

8. Your Social Security Number ___ – __ – ____

9. Your date of birth — MONTH / DAY / YEAR 19__

10. Your permanent telephone number — AREA CODE

11. Do you have a driver's license? **Yes** ○ 1 **No** ○ 2

12-13. Driver's license number and state — 12. LICENSE NUMBER | 13. STATE

14. Are you a U.S. citizen? Pick one. **See Page 2.**

- **a.** Yes, I am a U.S. citizen. ○ 1
- **b.** No, but I am an eligible noncitizen. **Fill in question 15.** ○ 2
- **c.** No, I am not a citizen or eligible noncitizen. ○ 3

15. ALIEN REGISTRATION NUMBER A________

16. Marital status as of today

- I am single, divorced, or widowed. ○ 1
- I am married. ○ 2
- I am separated. ○ 3

17. Month and year you were married, separated, divorced, or widowed — MONTH / YEAR

For each question (18 - 22), please mark whether you will be full time, 3/4 time, half time, less than half time, or not attending. Mark "Full time" if you are not sure. See page 2.

	Full time	3/4 time	Half time	Less than half time	Not attending
18. Summer 1999	○ 1	○ 2	○ 3	○ 4	○ 5
19. Fall semester or quarter 1999	○ 1	○ 2	○ 3	○ 4	○ 5
20. Winter quarter 1999-2000	○ 1	○ 2	○ 3	○ 4	○ 5
21. Spring semester or quarter 2000	○ 1	○ 2	○ 3	○ 4	○ 5
22. Summer 2000	○ 1	○ 2	○ 3	○ 4	○ 5

	Middle school/Jr. High	High school	College or beyond	Other/unknown
23. Highest school your father completed	○ 1	○ 2	○ 3	○ 4
24. Highest school your mother completed	○ 1	○ 2	○ 3	○ 4

25. What is your state of legal residence? STATE

26. Did you become a legal resident of this state before January 1, 1994? **Yes** ○ 1 **No** ○ 2

27. If the answer to question 26 is **"No,"** give month and year you became a legal resident. MONTH / YEAR

28. Most male students must register with Selective Service to get federal aid. Are you male? **Yes** ○ 1 **No** ○ 2

29. If you are male (age 18-25) and not registered, do you want Selective Service to register you? **Yes** ○ 1 **No** ○ 2

30. What degree or certificate will you be working towards during 1999-2000? **See page 2** and enter the correct number in the box.

31. What will be your grade level when you begin the 1999-2000 school year? **See page 2** and enter the correct number in the box.

32. Will you have a high school diploma or GED before you enroll? **Yes** ○ 1 **No** ○ 2

33. Will you have your first bachelor's degree before July 1, 1999? **Yes** ○ 1 **No** ○ 2

34. In addition to grants, are you interested in student loans (which you must pay back)? **Yes** ○ 1 **No** ○ 2

35. In addition to grants, are you interested in "work-study" (which you earn through work)? **Yes** ○ 1 **No** ○ 2

36. If you receive veterans' education benefits, for **how many months** from July 1, 1999 through June 30, 2000 will you receive these benefits?

37. **Amount per month?** $

For information purposes only. Do not submit.

For 38-52, if you are now married (even if you were not married in 1998), report both your and your spouse's income and assets. If you are not married, answer these questions about you and ignore the references to "spouse." If the answer is zero or the question does not apply to you, enter 0.

38. For 1998, have you filed your IRS income tax return or a tax return listed in **question 39**?

 a. I have already filed. ○ 1 **b.** I will file, but I have not yet filed. ○ 2 **c.** I'm not going to file. **(Skip to question 45.)** ○ 3

39. What income tax return did you file or will you file for 1998?

 a. IRS 1040 ○ 1 **c.** A foreign tax return. **See Page 2.** ○ 3

 b. IRS 1040A, 1040EZ, 1040Telefile ○ 2 **d.** A tax return for Puerto Rico, Guam, American Samoa, the Virgin Islands, Marshall Islands, the Federated States of Micronesia, or Palau. **See Page 2.** ○ 4

40. If you have filed or will file a 1040, were you <u>eligible to file a 1040A or 1040EZ</u>? **See page 2.** Yes ○ 1 No/don't know ○ 2

41. What was your (and spouse's) adjusted gross income for 1998? Adjusted gross income is on IRS Form 1040–line 33; 1040A–line 18; or 1040EZ–line 4. $ ☐☐ , ☐☐☐

42. Enter the total amount of your (and spouse's) income tax for 1998. Income tax amount is on IRS Form 1040–line 49; 1040A–line 32; or 1040EZ–line 10. $ ☐☐ , ☐☐☐

43. Enter your (and spouse's) exemptions. Exemptions are on IRS Form 1040–line 6d, and on Form 1040A–line 6d. For Form 1040EZ, **see page 2.** ☐☐

44. Enter your Earned Income Credit from IRS Form 1040–line 59a; 1040A–line 37a; or 1040EZ–line 8a. $ ☐ , ☐☐☐

45-46. How much did you (and spouse) earn from working in 1998? Answer this question whether or not you filed a tax return. This information may be on your W-2 forms, or on IRS Form 1040–lines 7, 12, and 18; or on 1040A–line 7; or on 1040EZ–line 1. You (45) $ ☐☐ , ☐☐☐

 Your Spouse (46) $ ☐☐ , ☐☐☐

47. Go to page 8 of this form; complete the column on the left of **Worksheet A**; enter student total here. $ ☐☐ , ☐☐☐

48. Go to page 8 of this form; complete the column on the left of **Worksheet B**; enter student total here. $ ☐☐ , ☐☐☐

49. Total current balance of cash, savings, and checking accounts $ ☐☐ , ☐☐☐

For 50-52, if net worth is one million or more, enter $999,999. If net worth is negative, enter 0.

50. Current <u>net worth</u> of <u>investments</u> (<u>investment value</u> minus <u>investment debt</u>) **See page 2.** $ ☐☐ , ☐☐☐

51. Current <u>net worth</u> of business (<u>business value</u> minus <u>business debt</u>) **See page 2.** $ ☐☐ , ☐☐☐

52. Current <u>net worth</u> of investment farm (Don't include a farm that you live on and operate.) $ ☐☐ , ☐☐☐

Step Two: If you (the student) answer "Yes" to any question in Step Two, go to Step Three.
If you answer "No" to every question, skip Step Three and go to Step Four.

53. Were you born before January 1, 1976? .. Yes ○ 1 No ○ 2

54. Will you be working on a degree beyond a bachelor's degree in school year 1999-2000? Yes ○ 1 No ○ 2

55. As of today, are you married? (Answer yes if you are separated, but not divorced.) Yes ○ 1 No ○ 2

56. Are you an orphan or ward of the court or were you a ward of the court until age 18? Yes ○ 1 No ○ 2

57. Are you a <u>veteran</u> of the U.S. Armed Forces? **See page 2.** .. Yes ○ 1 No ○ 2

58. Answer **"Yes"** if: (1) You have children who receive more than half of their support from you; **or**
 (2) You have dependents (other than your children or spouse) who live with you and receive more than half of their support from you, now and through June 30, 2000. Yes ○ 1 No ○ 2

Step Three: Complete this step only if you answered "Yes" to any question in Step Two.

59. How many people are in your (and your spouse's) <u>household</u>? **See page 7.** ☐☐

60. How many in question 59 will be <u>college students</u> between July 1, 1999, and June 30, 2000? **See page 7.** ☐

Now go to Step Five. (If you are a graduate health profession student, you may be required to complete Step Four even if you answered "Yes" to any questions in Step Two.)

For information purposes only. Do not submit.

Step Four: Please tell us about your parents. See page 7 for who is considered a parent.
Complete this step if you (the student) answered "No" to all questions in Step Two.

For 61 - 75, if the answer is zero or the question does not apply, enter 0.

61. For 1998, have your parents filed their IRS income tax return or a tax return listed in **question 62**?
   a. My parents have already filed. ○ 1
   b. My parents will file, but they have not yet filed. ○ 2
   c. My parents are not going to file. **(Skip to question 68.)** ○ 3

62. What income tax return did your parents file or will they file for 1998?
   a. IRS 1040 ○ 1
   b. IRS 1040A, 1040EZ, 1040Telefile ○ 2
   c. A foreign tax return. **See Page 2.** ○ 3
   d. A tax return for Puerto Rico, Guam, American Samoa, the Virgin Islands, Marshall Islands, the Federated States of Micronesia, or Palau. **See Page 2.** ○ 4

63. If your parents have filed or will file a 1040, were they eligible to file a 1040A or 1040EZ? **See page 2.** **Yes** ○ 1 **No/don't know** ○ 2

64. What was your parents' adjusted gross income for 1998? Adjusted gross income is on IRS Form 1040–line 33; 1040A–line 18; or 1040EZ–line 4. $ ___ , ___

65. Enter the total amount of your parents' income tax for 1998. Income tax amount is on IRS Form 1040–line 49; 1040A–line 32; or 1040EZ–line 10. $ ___ , ___

66. Enter your parents' exemptions. Exemptions are on IRS Form 1040–line 6d and on Form 1040A–line 6d. For Form 1040EZ, **see page 2.** ___

67. Enter your parents' Earned Income Credit from IRS Form 1040–line 59a; 1040A–line 37a; or 1040EZ–line 8a. $ ___ , ___

68-69. How much did your parents earn from working in 1998? Answer this question whether or not your parents filed a tax return. This information may be on their W-2 forms, or on IRS Form 1040–lines 7, 12, and 18; or on 1040A–line 7; or on 1040EZ–line 1.
   Father/Stepfather (68) $ ___ , ___
   Mother/Stepmother (69) $ ___ , ___

70. Go to page 8 of this form; complete the column on the right of **Worksheet A**; enter parent total here. $ ___ , ___

71. Go to page 8 of this form; complete the column on the right of **Worksheet B**; enter parent total here. $ ___ , ___

72. Total current balance of cash, savings, and checking accounts $ ___ , ___

For 73–75, if net worth is one million or more, enter $999,999. If net worth is negative, enter 0.

73. Current net worth of investments (investment value minus investment debt) **See page 2.** $ ___ , ___

74. Current net worth of business (business value minus business debt) **See page 2.** $ ___ , ___

75. Current net worth of investment farm (Don't include a farm that your parents live on and operate.) $ ___ , ___

76. Parents' marital status as of today? (Pick one.) Married ○ 1 Single ○ 2 Divorced/Separated ○ 3 Widowed ○ 4

77. How many people are in your parents' household? **See page 7.** ___

78. How many in question 77 will be college students between July 1, 1999, and June 30, 2000? **See page 7.** ___

79. What is your parents' state of legal residence? STATE ___

80. Did your parents become legal residents of the state in question 79 before January 1, 1994? **Yes** ○ 1 **No** ○ 2

81. If the answer to question 80 is "No," enter month/year for the parent who has been a legal resident the longest. MONTH ___ / YEAR ___

82. What is the age of your older parent? ___

For information purposes only. Do not submit.

Step Five: Please tell us which schools should receive your information.

For each school (up to six), please provide the federal school code and indicate your housing plans. Look for the federal school codes at your college financial aid office, at your public library, on the internet at http://www.ed.gov/offices/OPE, or by asking your high school guidance counselor. If you cannot get the federal school code, write in the complete name, address, city, and state of the college.

	Federal school code *OR* Name of college	College street address and city	State	Housing Plans
83.				**84.** on campus ○ 1 / off campus ○ 2 / with parent ○ 3
85.				**86.** on campus ○ 1 / off campus ○ 2 / with parent ○ 3
87.				**88.** on campus ○ 1 / off campus ○ 2 / with parent ○ 3
89.				**90.** on campus ○ 1 / off campus ○ 2 / with parent ○ 3
91.				**92.** on campus ○ 1 / off campus ○ 2 / with parent ○ 3
93.				**94.** on campus ○ 1 / off campus ○ 2 / with parent ○ 3

Step Six: Please read, sign, and date.

By signing this application, you agree, if asked, to provide information that will verify the accuracy of your completed form. This information may include a copy of your U.S. or state income tax form. Also, you certify that you (1) will use federal student financial aid only to pay the cost of attending an institution of higher education, (2) are not in default on a federal student loan or have made satisfactory arrangements to repay it, (3) do not owe money back on a federal student grant or have made satisfactory arrangements to repay it, and (4) will notify your school if you default on a federal student loan. If you purposely give false or misleading information, you may be fined $10,000, sent to prison, or both.

95. Date this form was completed.

MONTH ___ / DAY ___ / 1999 ○ or 2000 ○

96. Student signature

1 ____________________

Parent signature (one parent whose information is provided in Step Four.)

2 ____________________

If this form was filled out by someone other than you, your spouse, or your parent(s), that person must complete this part.

Preparer's Name and Firm ____________________

Address ____________________

97. Social Security # ___ – __ – ____

OR

98. Employer ID # __ – _______

99. Signature and Date 1 ____________________

SCHOOL USE ONLY

D/O ○ 1 Federal School Code

FAA Signature

1 ____________________

MDE USE ONLY

Special Handle _ – _______

For information purposes only. Do not submit.

Note that the first section of the FAFSA asks for general information such as name, address, social security number, your marital status, and so on. You will then be asked questions regarding your education (e.g., expected date of when you will receive your high school diploma) and your parents' educational background. Section C asks about your plans, for example, if you plan to enroll full-time or part-time in college, the degree you expect to receive, and the date you expect to receive it. You will be asked what type of financial aid you are interested in. Whether it's student employment, student loan, or parents' loans, check all of the listed options. Once you receive your offers, you can then decide which form of aid you prefer.

How you fill out section D will determine your student status, that is whether or not you are dependent or independent. You will have more financial aid options if you are independent. Section E asks for household information (how many people in your household attend college). Anyone who is taking at least 6 credits in your household should be counted.

Section F of the FAFSA form is where you answer questions regarding income and taxes. Since your W2s won't be ready for another month, use your return from the previous year.

In Section G your, parents report their investments, and in Section H, which colleges to send information. Finally, don't forget to sign your form. It is mandatory that you have a social security number and that you sign if you are considered an independent student, or you and your parents sign where indicated. The FAFSA cannot be processed without these steps taken.

Make sure that you make copies of everything before you send the FAFSA, whether it is by regular mail or e-mail.

A certain percentage of all FAFSAs filed each year are verified or audited. The Department of Education does this to make sure that the system stays honest. This is just another reason—it's also against the law—not to give misleading or false information on your FAFSA.

If you need help from the Department of Education filling out the FAFSA, the number to call is:

(800) 433-3243

For the hearing impaired:

(800) 730-8913 (TDD)

The profile

Some colleges want more information through the College Scholarship Services (CSS) Financial Aid Profile. This is also known as the Profile. A division of the College Board provides this form. The Profile should be submitted with the college admissions application. The Profile form is available from high school guidance counseling offices. The Profile is also available on-line for on-line submission. There is a charge for submitting the Profile. The participating colleges then use the data from both the FAFSA and the Profile to compute their financial aid package for your child. The College Board is the sponsor of the PSAT, SAT, TOEFL and CLEP exams and the AP program.

The Profile comes with an eight-page instruction booklet on how to fill out the form. Those instructions are also available with the on-line version (http://www.collegeboard.org).

The Profile asks for information based on the Federal Income Tax Form 1040, but in greater detail than the FAFSA.

Make sure that you make copies of everything before you send the Profile, whether it is by regular mail or e-mail.

In addition, some colleges require their own financial aid application, sometimes called the Family Financial Profile (FFP), in addition to the FAFSA and/or the Profile. This college financial aid application should also be submitted along with the college admissions application. These forms vary from college to college, but are similar to the Profile. They ask for financial information based on the Federal Income Tax Form 1040 in greater detail than the FAFSA.

Make sure that you make copies of everything before you send the FFP by regular mail with your application.

Free and not so free money

Scholarships

Work with your teen and your high school guidance department to begin research on scholarships for your child. There are many books available on this subject in addition to several scholarship search instruments on the Web. Pick the scholarships that seem to be a good fit for your child. Temper choices with the realization of the amount of work required by the college applications themselves, as well as the extra work required by the scholarship applications. Most scholarships will require the application, at least one essay, a resume, and family financial information.

Scholarships may be available for one year or the traditional four years. Now that it often takes students more than four years to complete their undergraduate work, it is a good idea to ask if the scholarship be renewed for a fifth year. Find out what are the requirements to renew the scholarship each year and if they have probationary terms in case of a poor academic semester, illness, or family crisis. Don't stop looking for new scholarships once your teen is in college. There may be departmental or degree-specific funds that be available.

If your child is academically talented, he/she may be eligible for your state's version of the "bright flight scholarship" or "brain drain scholarship". These scholarships are offered to students with certain academic qualifications as long as they go to colleges within their own resident state. Check with your guidance counseling office for forms, eligibility and residency requirements.

Scholarships based on physical talent (performing arts and sports) will require auditions, tapes and interviews. Check with each school and the specific department for requirements and deadlines. Please refer to the specialized sections later in this book.

College-based merit scholarships are scholarships offered by colleges to their top applicants based on academic and extracurricular achievement. These awards range from a few hundred dollars to a full scholarship, depending on the school. They may be for one year or for all four years. The competition for merit based scholarships is very stiff. The more selective the school is, the more competitive those top scholarships will be. Traditionally merit based scholarships at state universities are to benefit in-state resident students, but out-of-state students may also win these awards.

Independent scholarships

Sources for independent scholarships range from local service organizations and churches to employers, unions, and national corporations. Your high school guidance counseling office should have lists of scholarships available for your research. Keep in mind each of these will require its own application and the time to complete them. Some independent scholarships also have a large financial need component.

One of the most well known independent scholarship programs is the National Merit Scholarship Program sponsored by the National Merit Scholarship Corporation. This program is commonly referred to as the National Merit Program. The only way to obtain this scholarship is to take the PSAT exam in October of junior year.

If a student scores high enough, he/she will proceed to the next level of recognition. The basis for the recognition levels is the PSAT scores within each state. The first level of recognition is Commended. The next level is Semi Finalist. If a student is named a Semi Finalist, he/she will be required to fill out an extensive application and write an essay. He/she will also be required to take the SAT to provide additional substantiation of his/her academic achievement. If he/she scores beyond a certain level, he/she will be named a National Merit Finalist. A certain group of students, based on the scores, resume and essay, will advance beyond Finalist to be named National Merit Scholarship Corporation Scholars.

There is scholarship money potentially available for Semi Finalists, Finalists and Scholars. These scholarships range from a one-time award to a full scholarship for four years. It depends om which colleges your teen applies to.

Scholarships scams

Scholarship scams abound. Verify all information. If it seems too good, it probably is. Ask questions. Ask to see supporting documentation on the funding for the scholarship, if necessary.

Scholarship search companies

Be careful. Verify information. Ask questions. Keep in mind that no one can guarantee a scholarship. A company can locate scholarships for which your teen may be eligible, but cannot do anything beyond that. They cannot fill out the applications or apply for your teen.

Ask for the company's history. Check the company with the Better Business Bureau. Check the company against the listing of scholarship scams listed on the Federal Trade Commission's website (see Internet website boxes). If any company suggests that you change or amend your tax return, especially changing the tax status of your teen from dependent to independent, this should be a warning. Report the company immediately to the Justice Department, the IRS and the Federal Trade Commission. To falsify an income tax return for gain (such as for financial aid purposes) is illegal and punishable by fines and/or imprisonment.

Federal merit scholarship grants

Even the federal government plays a game with merit scholarship grants. They will award grants to students but might not fully fund the scholarship program or not fund it at all each year. Have backup plans available.

College credit in high school

One of the ways to possibly gain an advantage in lowering college cost is through taking college credit courses while in high school. This may shorten the time you spend in college.

Loans

Loans are what is available if the financial award from your teen's final college choice is short of what your family can handle from savings, investments, or on a current cash basis. The student with student loans graduates with an average of $13,500 in loans to repay.

Some states offer student loans. You will need to check with your state's Department of Higher Education to see if your state offers a loan program and for the details to apply.

The following is a list of the federal loan programs available at this time:

Student loans

Keep in mind that these programs are loans, which will have to be paid back at some point. Your lender is the Department of Education of the federal government. No matter what, do not default on your student loans. If you are running into difficulty, call the Department of Education and discuss the matter with them. There are options available if you run into trouble paying on time. Again, do not default on your federal student loans. The effect will be to ruin your credit rating, make you ineligible for any further federal student aid, prevent you from returning to college or graduate school, have your wages garnished and your federal income tax refund withheld, and possibly expose you to legal action by the federal government.

When you take out a federal student loan of any kind, you will sign a promissory note. In past years, you would sign a new note each time you took out a new loan. Now the school keeps a master promissory note on file that includes any federal student loan you receive for ten years. You will also be required to take part in an entrance interview before you sign your master promissory note which explains all of the loan specifics along with your rights and responsibilities as a federal loan borrower.

Keep copies of all of your loan documents in a safe place.

The Federal Direct Student Loan Program is federal loan money (such as the Stafford or the PLUS loans) distributed directly through your college. There are mandated limits of how much a student can borrow each year, but it can be no more than the amount of your demonstrated financial need.

COLLEGE BILL WOES

Never use money orders to pay student loans. Always use a check or bank cashier's check. This way, the bank will have a permamnent record of your payment. Money order companies will not.

The Federal Stafford Loan Program are loans to students from private sources such as banks, savings and loans associations, and so on. There are limits of how much a student can borrow each year, but it can be no more than the amount of your demonstrated financial need.

Annual Loan Limits are as of this writing:

First full year	$2,625
Second full year	$3,500
After second year	$5,500

For a college career total of no greater than $23,000 for dependent undergraduates and $46,000 for independent graduate students is permitted.

Both the Federal Direct Student Loans and the Federal Stafford Loans come in two options and a student may qualify to take out loans under both programs:

Subsidized

If the student has demonstrated (computed) financial need via the FAFSA, then the government pays the interest on the loan while he/she is in college. The interest rate is variable, but is capped at 8.25%. Repayment is deferred until six months after a teen graduates or leaves school. There is a loan origination fee and that amount is deducted from the loan amount before it is disbursed to your college.

Unsubsidized

If the student does not have demonstrated (computed) financial need via the FAFSA, or if the computed financial need has already been met through subsidized loans and/or scholarships, the student pays the interest throughout college, or the interest accumulates, until the principal payments come due after leaving college.

If a you transfer from one university to another, make sure you notify your loan provider of this change. Otherwise, your loan will be placed in repayment status and you will need to begin making payments. Other information you need to keep current is your name, permanent address, social security number and telephone number.

The Federal Work-Study Program is a campus-based program whereby the student works on campus, usually for the minimum wage. Depending on the financial aid award to the student, a portion of these funds are payable to the university.

The Perkins Loans is a campus-based program administered by participating colleges. This low-interest loan program is based on demonstrated need for both undergraduates and graduates with dire financial need. Currently, the maximum loan amount is $4,000 per year for undergraduates, for a total of $20,000 over the course of study. The grace period is nine months after you graduate or leave school.

Parent loans

Federal Parent Loans for Undergraduate Students, F(PLUS), are Federally based loans to parents to help finance their children's college undergraduate education. Parents may borrow up to the cost of education less any awards that have been given. Federal PLUS loans are given without regard to the computed financial need, but applicants must have a good credit history. Repayment must begin within 60 days of disbursement.

Direct PLUS are bank loans to parents for their children's college undergraduate education. Parents may borrow up to the cost of education less any awards that have been given. Direct PLUS loans are given without regard to the computed financial need

Home Equity Loans help to pay your child's college expenses. These loans are loans that are based on the equity you own in your home. The interest on these loans may qualify to be deducted on your federal income tax, if you meet the itemization requirements of the federal 1040 tax return. Consult your tax professional.

Note of caution: Be careful of leveraging your retirement income. Even though it is not considered as part of the computation of your assets by the FAFSA, it is by the Profile.

Grants

Grants are free monies that do not have to be repaid.

Federal Pell Grants depend on the EFC family computed level of contribution through the FAFSA and the college costs. Pell Grants are distributed based on how much the program has been funded for that year by Congress. The maximum grant per student is based on how much the Pell Grant program has been funded by the Congress for the next year. The funds come directly to the school and the college must notify you of how and when you or your school account will be paid.

Federal Supplemental Educational Opportunity Grant Program (SEOG) is a campus-based program for students beneath the poverty line. Again, the level of loans available depends upon Congressional funding of these programs each year. SEOG grants are not paid back and are only available for undergraduate education.

Grants to students now cover a lower percentage of the cost of attending college than several years ago. It appears that this trend will continue. Try to have back-up financing plans for future years in case you do not receive the same level of award/funding for your remaining college years.

Federal Work-Study (FWS) is a campus-based program that allows students to have jobs, usually on campus or in community service, to help pay for educational expenses. You must be paid at least once a month and at least at minimum wage.

Veterans' dependents benefits are for dependents of veterans killed or permanently disabled by a service-related injury. These dependents are eligible to receive a monthly award for education expenses. If you believe you are eligible, see your Veterans Administration Office.

Outside sources

Outside sources are often grandparents and/or other relatives or interested parties. These relatives and friends may hold the funds in an account until the student is ready for school. In computing financial aid awards, it is not always advisable for the student to hold large amounts in his/her own name. This decision should be made in consultation with your financial aid planner and/or tax professional.

Relatives and friends may also pay college fees (tuition, room, etc.) directly to the student's account at college and it does not come under the IRS $10,000 per year gift limitation rule. It does affect the FAFSA computations of demonstrated financial need or other financial needs-based computations and awards.

Tax programs

Effective with the 1998-99 academic year, there is the Hope Scholarship Credit. This is a federal tax credit of up to $1,500 per year for each student for the first and second years of college as long as a student is enrolled at least as a half-time student and meets other requirements.

For the remaining years of college, the student may take advantage of the Life Time Learning Tax Credit that applies to tuition and fees for undergraduate studies, continuing education and graduate studies. A student may take a tax credit of 20% of his/her educational expenses (tuition and fees) up to a maximum of $1,000 per year. The student needs to deduct all scholarships, grants and benefits before computing the Life Time Learning Tax Credit for the year. You need to check with the IRS or the Department of Education for further details on how these programs might affect you.

Tuition freezing

These are plans whereby the family agrees to pay the entire amount for four years of education at the beginning of the freshman year and the university will agree to freeze the amount due to a multiple of the first year's tuition. If a family has these financial resources, it saves the cost of the yearly increases in tuition, room and board. The drawback to this option is that the student may change schools partway through his college experience.

Monthly payment plans

Often, universities will contract with independent financing plans that allow parents to pay on a monthly or quarterly basis, interest free, for a small processing fee each year. This helps even out the payments rather than the lump sums due before each semester.

As with anything to do with the college process, you need to do your research so that your family makes sound, unhurried financial decisions. Start investigating and planning early in your child's high school career and then continually update and revise your plan. This format will give you the best chance of making good decisions at the lowest cost.

Options on lowering the costs and paying the bills

Loan forgiveness programs

Starting in late 1998, borrowers of new Stafford loans who serve as teachers in designated low-income schools may have up to $5,000 of their loans forgiven. The borrower must teach for five consecutive, complete school years. A similar program is available for child-care providers. But this program will not be enacted until Congress funds the loan forgiveness program.

Some states have a program of educational loan forgiveness based on teaching in low-income areas. Check with your state's Department of Higher Education to see if they have a program and what are the specifics.

Two-year colleges

Two-year colleges allow an additional flexibility in the journey to higher education. A two-year college can provide a terminal degree (Associate of Arts Degree—A.A.) in technical areas such as computers, 2-year nursing programs, electronics, etc. These degrees are designed so students are ready to go to jobs upon graduation. Often those technical programs also allow for training for people who are changing careers.

> "College is not the right option for every young person. If a hands-on, practical approach to learning appeals to you, you might explore the varied opportunities offered by technical school programs."
>
> Jill McM., High School College Career parapro

Two-year colleges also provide a starting point for students who perhaps did not have stellar high school careers or who need additional time to get ready for the transition to a four-year college.

Another advantage of a two-year college is the savings in money. Tuition at two-year colleges averages about half of what the average of the same years spent at a four-year college.

AmeriCorps

AmeriCorps is a national service program that provides education awards for a year or two of community service. For additional information, contact (800)942-2677 or on-line http://www.americorps.org

Cooperative education

These are programs within universities that allow students (usually upperclassmen) to work for a company in their field of study for a semester for pay and then return to school for a semester and still be considered a full time student in good standing.

College money use common sense tips

- *Buy used books whenever possible.*
- *Develop a budget.*
- *Use a checking account and balance your checkbook every month. Go to your bank or college credit union if you are experiencing difficulty.*
- *Watch out for over use of your ATM. There are charges associated with each withdrawal. Make sure you post them in your checkbook. Be careful when you withdraw money, especially at night.*
- *Don't use credit cards if at all possible. Save for true emergencies.*
- *Watch your phone bills. They can mount up in a hurry.*
- *Discount shop when you can.*

Financial aid on the Web

General financial aidinformation may be obtained on the World Wide Web. One of the biggest sites is the "FinAid: The Financial Aid Information Page" that is sponsored by the National Association of Student Financial Aid Administrators. (NASFAA). Their address (URL) is http://www.nasfaa.org

A link to FastWEB (Financial Aid Search Through the WEB) is supplied in the FinAid Web site. FastWEB is a database of tens of thousands of sources of financial aid and scholarships. It's free to users at http://www.fastweb.com

The FinAid home page gives links to every conceivable Web page dealing with financing your college education. In the navigation section, there is a link to a site named, "Mark's Picks". This site allows you to gain basic information and familiarity with some of the best websites available on financial aid. After you are comfortable with that information, you can then return to the main FinAid home page for more in depth information.

Within Mark's Picks, there are links to Web pages that provide calculators for financial aid. These calculators are all a little bit different, but when you use several of them, your results will give your family an idea of what their contribution will be as computed by the FAFSA.

THE INTERNET

The Department of Education's website has enormous financial aid information available at: http://www.ed.gov/

The College Board Online (CBO)'s Web site has a significant section on Financial Aid, including a Expected Family Contribution (EFC) estimators at: http://www.collegeboard.org

Another scholarship search engine is SRN Express at http://www.srnexpress.com

The online version of the Wintergreen/Orchard House Scholarship Finder is at: http://www.wgoh.com

You can also file your Free Application for Federal Student Aid (FAFSA) over the Internet at: http://www.fafsa.ed.gov. Filing electronically reduces the time for delivery of your Student Aid Report (SAR) with its vital figure for your Expected Family Contribution (EFC). But you still have to print out the signature page and mail it by conventional mail to the Department of Education before they can finalize your SAR. Filing electronically can save two to three weeks in processing time. Timing becomes an issue if your teen is going to be heavily dependent upon federal aid.

The Student Guide from the US Department of Education is available at: http://www.ed.gov/prog_info/SFA/StudentGuide/1999-0/intro.html

You can also file the College Scholarship Services (CSS) Financial Aid Profile (the Profile) via the Internet. Some colleges, in addition to the FAFSA, require the Profile. It is available through the College Board's Web site at: http://www.collegeboard.org

CASHE, is the independent scholarship search used by many universities. It is available at: http://www.cashe.com

Tax Program information is available at:
http://www.ed.gov/updates/97918tax.html

Scholarship Scam alerts: Watch out for scams, especially for financial aid search and scholarship. These scams abound. No one can truthfully promise to do all the work for you and guarantee you dollar awards. Go to the FTC's (Federal Trade Commission) website "Project $cholar $cam" for scam warnings:
http://www.ftc.gov/bcp/conline/edcams/scholarship/index.html

FinAid's Scam Alert provides useful information at:
http://www.finaid.org/scholarships/scams.html

6 Signs that Your Scholarship is Sunk at:
http://www.ftc.gov/bcp/conline/edcams/scholarship/sixsign.html is also a valuable resource.

Financial aid timeline at a glance

8TH Grade

- *Start mapping out your four-year financial plan including discussions with grandparents and others who may contribute funds towards college.*
- *Consult a financial planner, if necessary.*

9TH Grade

- *Begin the first year in your financial plan for college.*
- *Consult a financial planner, if necessary.*
- *Start general research on financial aid.*

10TH Grade

- *Start active research on scholarships.*
- *Implement the second year of your financial plan for college.*
- *Consult a financial planner, if necessary.*

11TH Grade

- *Implement the third year of your financial plan for college.*
- *Apply for any independent scholarships open to juniors.*
- *Start research into financial institutions that make educational loans.*
- *Attend financial aid workshops.*
- *In December, finalize any asset swapping that will be necessary for the most advantageous computation of*

financial need for financial aid awards. This needs to be accomplished by December 31st.

- *Initiate scholarship search making use of all sources including the Internet.*

12TH Grade

- *Apply to colleges and file any Profiles and individual college specific financial aid forms, as required.*
- *In November and December, obtain the FAFSA form from the high school guidance counseling office/counselor.*
- *Attend free college financial aid workshops.*
- *December, fill out the FAFSA as completely as possible.*
- *January, file the FAFSA using estimated tax document figures.*
- *February, receive the Student Aid Report (SAR) which is calculated from the FAFSA.*
- *As soon as possible, complete your Federal 1040 tax return and then re-file your updated SAR with the actual figures used in your and your teen's tax returns.*
- *February-March, receive corrected SAR based on actual tax return data.*
- *March-April, receive college financial aid notification (award letters) from all colleges to which you have been accepted.*
- *Compare all awards and proceed with any negotiations, if necessary.*
- *May 1st, finalize your decision and notify the colleges of that decision.*
- *May–July, apply for any loans needed.*

Highlights

★ Tuition is not the only college expense. There are other expenses to consider, such as room and board, books, travel, and personal needs. Keep these in mind when you figure out your financial situation.

★ Make sure you get a rough idea of your EFC. Once you have it figured out, the process of financial planning for your next four will be easier.

★ Every school wants a FAFSA and most schools want The Profile. You must fill these out and get them to the appropriate school on time, as soon after January 1st of your senior year as possible. This is the one thing you need to do if you want to be considered for financial aid.

★ There are many ways to lower the cost of going to college. Look into 2 year colleges, tuition freeze, and AmeriCorps, for example.

★ The Web has an invaluable amount of information on scholarships waiting for you.

★ There are many forms to fill out and deadlines to meet, just for financial aid. Make good use of the financial timeline so you don't miss or forget any part of this very important process.

Chapter 6

11th Grade

The Halfway Mark

- ✔ This is not a test, this is for real now
- ✔ Your top 10 colleges
- ✔ Calling all checklists
- ✔ College visits
- ✔ Get organized

This is not a test, this is for real now

Junior year. You've done a lot of planning. Now it's time to take action. If you haven't taken any of the college admissions tests (PSAT, PLAN, SAT I, ACT, TOEFL), you need to get started for the following reasons:

- *The more you can get done before your senior year, the better off you will be.*
- *If you need to take these tests (with the exception of the PSAT) more than once, you will have plenty of time to take them again. If you're not satisfied with your scores, you still have plenty of time to take a prep class and study more before taking them again.*

- *Your scores may also give you additional information to help you narrow down the list of colleges you're looking at.*

The PSAT, taken in the October of junior year, is necessary to become part of the National Merit and National Achievement Scholarship programs. This is another reason why you must take this test.

For most students, 11th grade is the time when the college admissions tests begin. There are several to take and you need to prepare for them in addition to your regular high school courses. This section builds on the test information in the 10th grade section of this book.

> "Take the ACT/SAT at least once your junior year and at least once your senior year."
>
> Cathe, student

> "Start early in your research. Attend college and financial aid fairs. If you take the SAT at least once during your junior year, you'll begin receiving college information to preview in your home."
>
> Cathy J., High School Learner Support Strategist

If you feel that you need help, there are courses available for the various exams. Check with your guidance counselor to see if your high school offers any of these. There are also companies that offer test prep courses for a fee.

If you have done well in your AP/IB courses, strongly consider taking those national exams in May. If you score high enough, you have the possibility of earning college credit for beginning freshmen courses.

Since most students do not know which college they will attend, they should take the SAT II (subject area) test for the AP/IB subject the spring or fall after taking the course. Check with the guidance office for further details and an application. A significant number of highly selective universities require these subject area (SAT II) tests regardless of other testing. Usually, students score better if taken right after course work has been completed.

If you have a disability, you will need to complete a student eligibility form obtained from your high school guidance counselor and provide current (within the last three years) diagnostic testing, evaluations, and comprehensive documentation with your application in order to have testing accommodations provided for your disability.

Registration and arrangement for these accommodations have to be set up well in advance. Because of the additional eligibility form, you cannot register for tests online or by fax.

Each testing service has special disability departments that handle these issues. Your high school guidance counseling office will handle these contacts for you. You need to follow through with your counselor to make sure the contacts were made and that you know exactly what is expected of you.

Examples of accommodations are wheelchair access, a sign language interpreter for spoken instructions, extended testing time, additional breaks, a scribe to record answers, a reader to dictate test questions, and other aids used in your daily life.

For a teen with a disability, a campus visit is imperative to meet with the people who will be your advocates, your help, and your mentors.

TESTING TIME LINE

Freshman	ACT and/or SAT I for practice, if warranted
Sophomore	
Fall	PSAT (Preliminary SAT) in October for practice
	PLAN (Preliminary ACT)
	SAT I
	ACT
Spring	SAT II (subject area tests), for practice
	AP (Advanced Placement) subject area tests, if warranted
Junior	
Fall	PSAT—actual, in October
	Only way into National Merit Scholarship programs
	SAT I
	ACT
	TOEFL, if appropriate
Spring	SAT II (subject area tests), if warranted
	AP(Advanced Placement) subject area tests, if warranted
	IB (International Baccalaureate) subject area tests, if warranted
Senior	
Fall	SAT I, if needed
	ACT, if needed
	TOEFL, if appropriate and needed
	SAT II (subject area tests), if needed for admission
	TWE (Test of Written English)
Spring	AP (Advanced Placement) subject area tests
	IB (International Baccalaureate) subject area tests

Your top 10 colleges

There are thousands of colleges in the United States and it seems that most of them have mailed you something in the last few months. Most likely, you have just ignored these mailings. Now it's time to do something about them.

> "I would recommend starting your college hunt at the end of your junior year. Start applying for scholarships and scheduling college visits. It's never too early to get a jump start on your future."
>
> Misty, student

Keep in mind that everything that comes to you by mail is a form of marketing. These materials won't give you any negative information about the college. How do you find this out? Don't worry, as you investigate and research, you will discover the warts.

The first thing you need to do is ask yourself some questions and set some goals.

- *What do you want to do?*
- *What do you enjoy studying?*
- *What part of the country do you want to be in?*
- *How far from home do you want to go?*

These are just the tip of the iceberg of possible questions you might ask yourself. (If you need a refresher on how to set goals, refer to the goal setting portion of the 8th grade section of this book.)

Some people view college as a way to learn skills for your careers. If you are inclined to do this, you will need to decide what type of career you hope to have once you are out of college. Then try and match your career goals with a major or concentration of study. This is very difficult to do. Many students don't even decide on a major until the beginning of their junior year in college.

Most kids also change their majors at least once while in college. If you have chosen a college for one major and that is the only thing that has attracted you to that school, you may have to change schools to change your major.

> "My main piece of advice for looking for a college is make sure that you research the college before applying. Is it something that will fulfill your long-term career objectives? How is the college ranked nationally for the degree program that you are interested in pursuing?"
>
> Misty, student

> "Don't rely solely on your high school advisors for school planning, scholarship endeavors, etc."
>
> Cathe, student

PARENTS CORNER

Going to school close to home usually brings down the cost of college because of reduced transportation costs. This is something to consider if there are financial constraints.

> "Consider location carefully. After high school, people have a tendency to want to get as far away from parents as possible. However, many students get far away and realize that the sudden change is too much and they end up going home, which could cause problems later. Some students do well far away, but thinking it over seriously is a good idea."
>
> Dana, student

> "Do not feel pressured by the idea that you need to get away from home in searching for the most appropriate school. The inside of the lecture hall, the space between lines n a book, the openness around an idea, and the width and breadth of the new found camaraderie at your

> college will be millions of miles from where you are now. Remember—it is not where you start, but where you finish that makes the difference in your life."
>
> Randy C., teacher

Another criterion for college choice today is the level of technology available for students on campus. Samples of technologies available on campuses include:

- *High speed Internet access connections in dorm room (not by phone line);*
- *Offering special dialing-in services for students living off campus;*
- *On-line library research via campus network;*
- *Web-based course and research assignments via the campus network and professors' own Web pages;*
- *Out-of-class contact between student and professor via e-mail;*
- *Network plug-ins for notebook computers in classrooms;*
- *On-line course registration*

Even though 80% of students come with their own computers, computers should also be available in computer labs, the library, and in student centers. Students need to be able to work anywhere on campus, not just in their dorm room or in the library. You also will need to know what type of computers will interface best with your campus network.

Some universities have made research part of every core course and have established minimum requirements for the percentage of research to be found from the Internet.

In the final list of schools, there may be a couple of schools, which would very expensive and difficult to get into. These are schools which you would attend if you were accepted and scholarships were available. Obviously, your final list should not consist entirely of these schools.

Your final list of schools should also include a couple of schools that are good matches for you academically and financially. This is your realistic group. There also should be one or two schools that you know you will be accepted to and can afford. This will be your well-rounded list of schools to apply.

If medical school is possibly in your future, determine if the colleges you are applying to:

- Are affiliated with a medical school and hospital.
- Have an automatic feed option from their undergraduate program to their medical school. (An automatic feed means that as long as you fulfil requirements and your collegiate grades are at least at the minimum, you get into the med school.)
- Have volunteer options available for undergraduates at hospital.
- Have working options for undergraduates at hospital and medical school.
- Have research options for undergraduates at a hospital and/or medical school.

If the college is not affiliated with a medical school or hospital, find out if arrangements have been made with a medical facility for students who are in the Pre-Med program for:

- Volunteer work
- Shadowing experiences
- Working options
- Research options

These options are important, because if medical school is truly your goal, then, in addition to top collegiate grades and top MCAT scores, you have to have hospital-based/oriented volunteer, work, and/or research experience.

To Ivy League or not, to highly selective schools or not

Ivy League Schools are not the only schools that will allow you to receive an incredibly good education. There are many selective/highly selective universities that will accomplish the same or similar goals for you.

Analyze your personality and drive carefully. Ask for adult input on this. Generally, if you choose a highly selective college and to be fully successful throughout your college career; you must not only have high grades and test scores for admission, but you must also have high self-esteem and a strong self-image. You will no longer be one of a handful of the best students in the high school population, but just one of an entire all-poweful first year class at the university.

It is a mental game. If you can understand prior to attending that you may not be one of the top in your college class and most probably will not make the top grades, there is a much greater chance of success. This is an important consideration in your final college choice.

Some advantages of choosing a selective/highly selective university are: chances for funded undergraduate research, internships, networking and mentoring relationships with nationally/internationally renowned professors, and increased chances for study and/or work abroad experiences as an undergraduate.

To combat "brain drain" or "bright flight" states are offering top students scholarships, grants, job placement services, etc. These special scholarships are to keep these kids in-state for school. Why? About 70% of students who leave their state to go to college do not come back to work.

Calling all checklists

So, you've figured out what types of colleges you are interested in. You may even have some specific colleges in mind. Your next step is to do a little investigating. Search the Internet and the college's handbook, talk to your friends, and family, and then fill in the checklist below. If there are any questions you can't find the answer to, ask the admissions office.

Using the college call checklist

Use the information from your completed College Call Checklists to make a small database using the information most important to you. Sort your information based on the most significant criteria and print the results. It helps to filter your top 20 choices to the intermediate 10-12 and then finally down to the top six. Sometimes this process helps clear the picture for you.

COLLEGE CALL CHECKLIST

COLLEGE NAME ______________________________

Contact person

Phone number:

Fax number:

Internet address:

Admissions address

ENTRANCE REQUIREMENTS:

High School courses required?

Which college admissions tests are required?

How many students are in these specialties?

FRESHMAN CLASS:

What is typical freshman schedule like?

What is the retention rate for freshman?

What are average SAT/ACT scores for in-coming freshmen?

What percent of graduates go onto Graduate School?

Do graduate students teach freshmen?

What is the percentage of class who graduates in 4 years?

What is percentage of class who takes 5+ years to complete undergraduate work?

APPLICATION INFO:

Application method:

Traditional paper application?

Included in View Book?

Internet download application?

Internet on-line application?

On-Disk application? Any extra fees involved?

Which application method does university prefer?

Does university allow use of The Common Application?

(Continued)

Essay required with application?

How many?

Deadline(s) for application

Application fee, how much?

University-specific Financial Aid Estimator included?

LIBRARY:

What are the library's hours?

Computerized book catalog?

Networked to any out6side library resources?

RANKINGS:

U.S. News & World Report

The Gourman Report

Money Magazine

INTERDISCIPLINARY STUDIES

Available?

Are the programs within specific curriculum areas, such as in sciences?

(Or) Across all programs

(Or) University defined

Degree available

OPTIONS FOR UNDECIDED MAJORS

Special academic counseling?

Special mentoring available?

EXTRACURRICULAR ACTIVITIES

What are the athletic and recreational facilities available?

Sports: intramural, club

Sports, varsity (Consult student's high school coach(s) for specific information/methods of seekingt athletic scholarships: e.g.: references, play videos, etc.)

Orchestra/Band for music/non-music majors

Theater for theater/non-theater majors

(Continued)

COMPUTER INFORMATION

IBM or Mac-based?

Campus networked:

Dorm rooms networked?

Through phone lines or direct network cabling in room?

Internet connection capabilities?

Computer labs

Location and how many?

What are hours of operation?

CAMPUS INFO

Population

If this is a rural area, how far is it to the nearest city and how do students get there?

Where is the closest major airport to campus?

What is the percentage of Greek life (Fraternities and Sororities) on campus?

What method of transportation do students use to get around campus?

What are the regulations for freshman regarding cars?

Does the university have its own bus system and what are its hours of operation?

Health services available?

HOUSING IN GENERAL

- Voice Mail available?
- Single-sex dorms available?
- Coed dorms, how structured?
- Freshman segregated?
- What is supplied in dorm rooms? Can you use lofts?
- Where are Laundromats?
- How are roommates assigned?
- Refrigeration rental?
- Are there smoke free rooms/dorms available?
- Is air conditioning available for students who have certified medical needs, i.e. severe allergies, asthma, etc.?

(Continued)

MEAL PLANS

- How many meals available per day and on which days? (Some universities only offer an evening meal.)
- What are the other food options available on campus?

PROSPECTIVE STUDENT VISITS:

Days and hours

Special weekends

Arranged?

Special places to stay near or on campus?

Campus map?

Map of area?

TUITION AND FINANCIAL AID

Tuition

Room and Board

Fees, miscellaneous and books

Any tuition-ceiling guarantee programs available?

Which forms are needed for financial aid?

Deadline(s)

When are deposits due for freshmen (a.k.a. First Years)?

How much?

What types of payment plans are available?

Is this a state-supported university:

How much are the out-of-state fees?

Does that state have a reciprocity agreement with yours, whereby those out-of-state fees may be waived?

Are there any circumstances in which the out-of-state fees may be waived?

I'm honored

Honors Programs allow you to work at high academic levels. Honors classes tend to be small, in-depth, specialized and often they are taught by the top professors of the university.

Entrance into an Honors program is university determined. The criteria can range from a matrix of GPA/test scores to a specialized competitive application process.

Some Honors programs have Honors housing (whether in a separate dorm or floor) that allow Honors students to live and study together as a close-knit community. Another housing option includes grouping by degree interest.

There are some perks besides smaller classes of belonging to an Honors Program. Honors students are often offered increased and earlier opportunities for student research. Some colleges allow Honor students to register early, thus getting the pick of the courses, schedules, and professors. Other perks can include specialized counseling, study rooms, social activities, and the opportunity to work with the best students in the school.

Honors Programs have specialized courses that you will be required to take. In some programs, these courses are substitutes for core curriculum degree requirements. One problem with these courses is that they are so specialized that they will often not transfer as required core curriculum courses to another college. This will be important if you decide to change universities.

In other Honors programs, the required Honors courses are in addition to the degree required course work. If you have an intensive degree program, this type of Honors program will add to your already heavy workload.

Some universities only offer departmental Honors while others offer general Honors programs.

Most Honors programs require some type of capstone project during the senior year. If your degree program requires a senior project, often this can be used as the Honors project with some additional criteria.

If a student successfully completes the requirements of the Honors Program, there will be a notation of it on the degree and transcript.

COLLEGE CALL CHECKLIST

HIGH ACADEMICS AND HONORS OPTIONS

Within specialized programs for scholars is there:

- Specialized counseling?
- Special mentoring with top faculty/administrators?
- What are the research opportunities for top scholars?
- Available for underclassmen?
- What are special provisions made for upperclassmen?
- Is there research funding for undergraduates?
- What mentoring programs are available?
- What are the summer opportunities for top scholars?

Scholarship Information

Merit based scholarships

- Requirements for awarding and maintaining
- Award specifics
- Essay required?
- Deadline(s) for submission
- GPA required for renewal

Premier scholarship?

- Requirements for awards
- Profile of typical recipients of this award
- Award specifics
- Interview day/weekend required?
- Have scholarship application?
- Essay required?
- Deadline(s) for scholarship application
- GPA required for renewal
- Is there a specialized scholars group based in the awardees of this scholarship?

Honors Program Information

- How many students are involved in the program

(Continued)

Is admission to the program competitive or won the basis of GPA or SAT/ACT scores?

Structure of program

Are required Honors courses in lieu of core curricula

Or

In addition to core curricula

Are Specialized honors core courses transferable as core curricula to other universities?

Separate Housing either by Honors designation or by degree interest?

Is there a cummunity service component?

ADVANCED WORK CREDIT:

Advanced placement/International Baccalalureate classes:

Have conversion chart to send?

What is the minimum score required for credit to count?

Cap on hours, which can transfer?

Transfer with grade?

Go toward degree requirements

Number of transferable hours based on your tests and scores

Dual Enrollment/College credit classes, *i.e.:* 1-8-1-8 classes taught at high school or taking class(es) at college while still in high school?

Transfer?

Transfer with grade?

College correspondence classes

Transfer?

Transfer with grade?

Performing arts

For those of you looking to dance, sing, or act your way through the next four years, the checklist for performing arts is different. The performing arts disciplines have some common elements and then each has its own specialized questions.

The following pertains to the performing arts:

- *Attend specialized college fairs for the performing arts. Check with your guidance counselor for dates and sites.*
- *Participate in summer programs and get letters of recommendation from your teachers and coaches.*
- *Take private lessons if at all possible.*
- *Participate in honors and/or metropolitan or regional choruses, bands, orchestras, dance troupes or theater productions as your schedule allows.*
- *Apply early—this will possibly allow you to get your pick of audition dates.*
- *Research and apply for specialized scholarship programs and official recognition programs.*
- *For dance and musical theater, work on injury prevention through conditioning programs and nutrition. If you have been injured, you need to be honest with the college.*
- *Keep in mind that being the top in your high school does not necessarily translate to being the top in college.*

Auditions and interviews will require:

- *Two solos from a standard list if for vocal or instrumental or musical theater.*
- *For instrumental music, excerpts from orchestral selections, especially for conservatories.*
- *For instrumental music, all scales (major and minor).*
- *For percussionists: Prepare pieces for mallets, timpani, snare drum, and accessory percussion (tambourines, triangle, etc.).*

- *For drama and musical theater, a monologue of your choice from memory.*
- *For drama and musical theater, required monologues from memory.*
- *For drama and musical theater, a cold reading.*
- *For musical theater, one or two selections from musical theater. Pick them to be of contrasting styles.*
- *Conservatories may have additional/substitute requirements.*
- *Programs from your high school career, especially if you were a featured soloist, lead or dancer.*
- *Keep a portfolio/file on everything and have copies ready to present at your audition, etc.*
- *Expect to sight-read if for vocal, instrumental or musical theater.*
- *Some schools may require a written theory exam.*
- *There may be local auditions—check, it may save you a trip.*
- *Be ready to audition by the first week in February (ranges from late January through March) [or through May for some dance programs].*
- *Check with each school and see if taped and/or video-taped auditions are allowed.*
- *Auditions are often videotaped (especially for dance and musical theater), just ignore the camera.*
- *For dance and musical theater, prepare thoroughly before the audition in your dance class and by constructing your solo (if requested) based on the instructions given in your audition packet.*
- *For dance and musical theater, some auditions are actually your participation in classes on campus the day of auditions. Prepare in your dance class based on the instructions given in your audition packet.*
- *For vocal, musical theater or dance, verify if there will be an accompanist available for audition or if you will need a tape accompaniment.*

- *For dance, you will probably need a full-length photo in dance attire.*
- *For drama, you will probably need a head shot photograph.*

Auditions

- *Arrive one hour early.*
- *Don't chew gum.*
- *Dress appropriately—simply (or follow instructions in your audition letter).*
- *For dance, dress appropriately and bring changes of clothes and dance shoes according to the audition requirements. Hair should be out of your face.*
- *For drama, dress appropriately, usually in simple black.*
- *For musical theater, dress appropriately and bring changes of clothes and shoes for each segment—voice, drama and dance.*
- *For vocal and instrumental, bring copies of sheet music.*
- *For drama and musical theater, bring copies of monologues.*
- *For dance and musical theater, bring copies of taped accompaniment or music for pianist.*
- *Bring copies of audition schedule letter.*
- *Bring any equipment you will need.*
- *Bring water and/or cup.*
- *Bring your portfolio and copies.*
- *For dance and musical theater, bring any health forms required.*
- *For dance and musical theater, bring any equipment and extra clothing you will need.*
- *When you pick out your literature, select something that showcases your voice or body, and your talents, but don't select something that is totally out of reach—only sets up your audition for a less than stellar performance.*

- *For instrumental music, drama and musical theater work on your position, presentation and style.*

COLLEGE CALL CHECKLIST

(This is only a guide. This provides a framework for each family to verify and personalize.)

PERFORMING ARTS

What is the enrollment in this program?

Video portolio required?

For drama, how many different events should be included?

Audiotape or video-taped portfolio required?

How long in minutes?

How many different events should be included?

Auditions required?

Live or videotaped?

When are these held and where?

Who judges the auditions?

How many performances are required per year?

Where are your alumni performing now and/or which troupes are they members?

What are the professional credentials of your teaching staff?

For dance and musical theater, what are the professional credentials of your choreographer(s)?

What are the casting policies in school plays, musicals, etc.?

For dance and musical theater, given the emphasis on thinness in the dance world, does the program have a policy on weight? If so, what is it?

For dance and musical theater, what is the flooring in the dance studios?

(Continued)

COLLEGE CALL CHECKLIST

(This is only a guide. This provides a famework for each family to verify and personalize.)

PERFORMING ARTS—(Continued)

For dance and musical theater, how many dance studios are available?

For instrumental music, how many rehearsal studios are there?

- What are the required extracurricular activities, if any?
- For drama and musical theater, which Thespian Societies are on campus?

The art of it...

For those of you looking to paint, draw, and sculpt, the rules of the game are a little different as well.

- *Attend specialized College Art Fairs - check with your guidance counselor for dates and sites.*
- *Experiment with a variety of mediums, black & white and color.*
- *Do still life's, abstracts and work from your imagination.*
- *Do NOT copy photographs - this is rendering and not a skill desired in your work for admission.*
- *Portfolio work for the college interview process must be from the previous two years.*
- *Try and enroll in a summer art program between the junior and senior years.*

Attend a National Portfolio Day at a college to have your portfolio reviewed. If you attend one during your junior year, you should also try to attend one early in your senior year to help prepare you for your portfolio interviews. Your high school visual arts teacher will be able to give you dates and places.

Besides a certain level of skill and talent, the characteristic that contributes to success in the college art world is your dedication to your craft. It is not good enough just to do an assignment. It is your passion to be the best you can be in all media's which entails intense dedication and risk taking.

There is the question of majoring in visual arts in a university vs. art institute setting. For some students, working in an art institute is the choice. An art institute allows for total immersion in all forms of art in the beginning and the specialty as an upperclassman. For other students, a college setting offers some diversity to the day and to the awarded degree in terms of course offerings, students and faculty.

COLLEGE CALL CHECKLIST

(This is only a guide. This provides a framework for each family to verify and personalize.)

VISUAL ARTS

Portfolio required for admission to art department or school?

What medium's?

What styles?

Slides for portfolio:

How many slides are required?

How should the slides be marked?

Will they be returned?

Deadline for portfolio for admission to art department or school?

Portfolio required for scholarship at art department or school?

Deadline for portfolio for scholarship at art department or school?

Portfolio interview required for scholarship at art department or school?

Senior Show required for degree?

Does the Senior Show count for credit hours toward graduation?

Are there undergraduate art shows at the college?

Sports and college admissions

Athletic ability can help you get into the college of your choice. It can even be the starting point for a fabulous professional career. To play college sports anywhere, keep in mind that college coaches are looking for superior athletes. You might be the best at your high school or maybe even in your region, but you still may not be good enough to play at the collegiate level.

You need to determine if you are of the right size to play your sport at the college level. Coaches look for size and speed.

You need to be strong to play at the college level. Keep in good physical shape—even in the off-season. Work with a trainer, if necessary. You also need to be mentally tough to play.

You always need to keep in mind that your primary goal in going to college is to get an education. Athletics is a means to the end result of a college degree. Your goal has to be to graduate from college. Why? Because so very few kids make it to the pros. If you do make it to the pros, no matter how gifted an athlete you are, there will come a time when you will no longer be able to play your sport. You have to build the foundation for a time after sports. One of blocks of that foundation is a college degree. Therefore, you have to work hard, go to your classes, complete your assignments, and turn them in. You need to study for tests and you need to pass them. You need to get from your first semester to your last.

Set priorities and goals for yourself. General priorities should be (in this order): academics, extracurricular activities, and a social life. If you keep them in that order, you will be successful and graduate. Learn to manage your time well. You will need to be able to do that during pre-season and when you are juggling practices, games, extensive travel, and lack of sleep along with your school work. Work on your study skills so that you discover the best and easiest way to learn. Don't be afraid to ask for help. Keep in mind that if your grades drop too far, you won't be eligible to play.

Playing a sport in college is a time to make great memories and friends. Be a good friend. Always act your best—no matter what any sports writer writes, how you played, or the bad call by the refs. Always think about how you want to remember yourself during your college years.

Read all the materials you are sent. Fill out any questionnaires sent to you by coaches and mail them back promptly. Make sure you make copies of everything. At the beginning, don't rule out any school. You don't know enough yet to know which one will be "the one".

Involve your high school and coaches to help you negotiate the sports application process. They can send out requested videos for you and make phone calls on your behalf. Ask for a letter of recommendation, but don't do it during the season. Let your coach know which colleges you are considering. But keep in mind that you aren't the only student he or she is helping. Be prompt in your requests. Give your coach as much information as possible, and then follow up with the coach to make sure everything was done in a timely manner.

You will need a specialized resume that should include education, academic achievements, extracurricular activities, community service, athletics, academic and athletic references, your intended major, and your athletic goals. (Refer to resume section of the 9th grade chapter of this book.)

Contact coaches at the colleges you are interested in as soon as possible. Coaches want to know if you are interested. You must show a genuinely serious interest in that college. Don't waste the coach's time or your own on a whim. If a coach has contacted you but you don't have an interest in that school, don't be afraid to tell the coach.

Start your investigations early. You have a lot of ground to cover. Start your unofficial college visits as early as sophomore year. (Unofficial visits are ones that you and your family pay for.)

If at all possible, go to summer camps in your sport. These camps help you hone your skills, keep you in shape, demonstrate your dedication, and enable you to compete against top players in your sport. Also, the camp coaches are often university coaches.

There are recruiting services available for a fee. Check their references and be aware of possible fraud. Some student-athletes have Web pages made about their athletic qualifications. There are firms that will do this for you and send them to specific colleges. There are fees involved in this service.

Videotape has become an important part of athletic recruiting. This is especially true if your high school has not had a good record or you come from a small town that isn't visited by college athletic recruiters or coaches.

If your high school videotapes, ask if you can have a copy made of particular games. If your family has a video camera, ask your parents or a friend to tape you at most of your games. Your final tape should have a 10-minute block of a single game. The rest of the tape should be highlights from other games and a run-through of your basic skills and moves. Try to have the video show you using several different play skills.

Make sure there is an introduction on the tape, with the student's name, high school, high school coach's name, telephone numbers, and addresses. Put a label on the outside of the tape with the student's and high school's names and phone numbers.

Make copies of the video from a master tape. Send the copies out. Never send your master.

Don't send out an unsolicited video to a college coach unless you are really interested in the school. In most cases, you will not get your video back. Include a letter of introduction and your resume.

Always follow-up with a coach you sent information. A stat sheet may be asked for from time-to-time. If a college has a sincere interest in a student, they will call the high school coach.

Due to your athletic schedule, it might take you five years to get through college rather than the traditional four years.

Be sure to check with your high school athletic activities director so your school's programs don't suffer because of unauthorized contacts of individual athletes who are still in high school.

Check the college play schedule for your sport against the regular college calendar. Are you prepared to be separated from your family during Thanksgiving or other holidays because of team practice?

The National Collegiate Athletic Association (NCAA)

For the top level of college sports, the NCAA rules strictly govern the interaction between college coaches and prospective student players. Check often with your guidance counselor and your high school coach for the current NCAA regulations. There are reference books available to help you through the process. Since the NCAA guidelines constantly change, you need to keep current with the latest version. Use your coaches and the NCAA itself as resources.

If you want to compete at the NCAA Division I or II level, you must register with the NCAA clearinghouse for freshman year eligibility. Forms are sent to high schools after August 1st of every year. The form is good through June 30th after senior year. There is a small fee for this service which can be waived in cases of financial hardship. You should register, at the very latest, at the beginning of senior year. If you play a fall sport, then at the very latest, you need to register toward the end of junior year. You cannot make an official recruiting visit to a college unless you are registered with the NCAA clearinghouse.

Remember individual schools may have additional requirements besides those of the NCAA.

Beginning in 1999, the courts have prohibited the NCAA from using the SAT or the ACT scores as part of the academic eligibility requirements for athletes to participate in an NCAA sport. The NCAA has asked the courts to postpone this ruling until their appeal has been heard and a decision rendered.

As of this writing, this situation is unresolved.

Contact the NCAA for any questions or concerns you may have regarding these issues and the academic eligibility requirements.

When you graduate from high school, if you do not meet the academic eligibility requirements (however they are defined), consider attending a junior college for two years and earn an A.A. degree to give yourself time to improve your grades and your athletic skills and experience. Some junior colleges are known for producing great athletes within a certain sport. Contact the National Junior College Athletic Association for further information.

Academic eligibility requirements, Division I

(based on the requirements before the 1999 Court ruling banning ACT/SAT scores)

- *During high school you need to pass the following courses*

  4 years of English
  2 years of Math (1 in Algebra and 1 in Geometry)
  2 years of social science
  2 years of natural or physical science (1 being lab course)
  1 additional year of math, English, or science
  2 additional courses in an academic area

- *You need to be a high school graduate*
- *You need to have at least a 2.500 (out of 4.000) GPA and a minimum sum of the test section scores on the ACT of 68 and the SAT of 820 (SAT after 4/1/95). There is an eligibility sliding scale of GPA and ACT/SAT—Please consult the NCAA for details.*

Division II, NCAA colleges

- *Athletic budgets and facilities below the standards to compete at Division I.*
- *Over 200 schools participate*
- *Offer athletic scholarships, but not at the quantity of Division I schools*
- *No alumni or boosters may be part of your recruiting process.*
- *You (or your family) may not receive anything (monetary or physical) that would be considered a bribe to play sports at that school*
- *Athletic recruitment letters may not start before 9/1 of your junior year.*
- *Phone calls—not till after mid-summer after junior year*

  (check NCAA for specific date each year)
  no more than 1 call per week, except

5 days before your official visit to college
Day of off-campus visit with coach
Initial date for signing National Letter of Intent
and the 2 following days

Football has different regulations—

Usually starting earlier than the above regulations
(Check with NCAA for specific dates each year)

- *Contacts*
  After July 1st following junior year
  No more than 3 times off campus (except in football—7 times)
  Cannot visit high school more than once a week
- *Evaluations*
  Used to assess your qualifications to play
  Limited number of visits per year
  (Check with NCAA for specifics)
- *Official Visits*
  Senior year
  Expenses paid
  One per college
  No more than 5 colleges
  College has to have your high school transcript and test scores

Academic eligibility requirements, Division II

(based on the requirements before the 1999 Court ruling banning ACT/SAT scores)

- *During high school you need to pass the following core courses (not remedial or vocational)*
  3 years of English
  2 years of Math (1 in Algebra and 1 in Geometry)
  2 years of social science
  2 years of natural or physical science (1 being lab course)
  2 additional year of math, English, or science
  2 additional courses in an academic area
- *You need to be a high school graduate*
- *You need to have at least a 2.000 (out of 4.000) GPA and a minimum sum of the test section scores on the*

ACT of 68 and the SAT of 820 (SAT after 4/1/95). There is an eligibility sliding scale of GPA and ACT/SAT—Please consult the NCAA for details.

Division III, NCAA colleges

- *Over 350 schools participate*
- *Athletics and academics share time, instead of athletics taking predominance over academics*
- *Generally do not give athletic scholarships*
- *Offer financial aid*
- *You (or your family) may not receive anything (monetary or physical) that would be considered a bribe to play sports at that school*
- *You may not tryout for an athletic team*
- *Contacts*
  After your junior year
  No limits on number or timing
- *Official Visits*
  Senior year
  Expenses paid
  One per college
  Unlimited if you initially enrolled at Div III school
  College has to have your high school transcript and test scores

National letter of intent: institutional or conference

- *The letter is administered by the Collegiate Commissioners Association.*
- *If you have questions, ask the conference where your college belongs.*
- *Each sport has a range of dates when it is permitted to sign the letter.*
- *Don't sign any Letter before the permitted signing date for your sport.*

In a NCAA school, eligibility starts when you begin school. The student has five years in which to use four years of eligibility. The five years are consecutive.

Other options outside the NCAA

Prep schools

- *Offer an interim step between high school and college for one year.*
- *They provides extra time for academic preparation as well as for athletic preparation.*
- *They are relatively expensive.*

Junior colleges

- *Do not require a specific ACT or SAT score for acceptance.*
- *They offer an interim step between high school and college for to two years (the time needed to earn an AA degree).*

- *They provides extra time for academic preparation as well as for athletic preparation.*
- *They are relatively inexpensive.*

National Association of Intercollegiate Athletics (NAIA)

- *Tend to be small schools*
- *About 400 schools participate*
- *Limited sports programs*
- *Financial aid is available*
- *In the NAIAA a student has ten semesters of eligibility and can be any time during one's college career.*

Academic Eligibility Requirements, NAIA

(Meet two out of three as a minimum)

- *Minimum score of 18 on ACT or 740 combined SAT*
- *Minimum GPA of 2.000 (out of 4.000)*
- *Graduate in the upper half of your high school graduating class*

National Small College Athletic Association (NSCAA)

- *Small schools (under 1000 students)*
- *About 100 schools participate*

Sports websites

National Collegiate Athletic Association

NCAA website (Guide for college bound):

http://www.ncaa.org

National Junior College Athletic Association

NJCAA (Junior Colleges) website:

http://www.njcaa.org

National Association of Collegiate Directors of Athletics (NACDA):

http://www.nacda.com

National Scouting Report:

http://www.nsr-inc.com

National Recruiting Center (NRC)

http://www.nrc.pair.com

Athletic Scholarship Information Search Techniques (Sports A.S.I.S.T)

http://www.athletes.com

American Sport Education Program

http://www.asep.com

A special note to female athletes

Take special care and preparation of your knees. As more young women play sports, the rate of increase in females in injuries to the anterior cruciate ligament (ACL) have increased dramatically in comparison to males. The current thinking in the field of biomechanics is that the situations for the injuries are set up are due to the differences between the sexes in the structure of the pelvis and knee. The muscle structure in the legs also differs between males and females.

This is not an argument for women to stop playing sports. It is a warning to young women to take extra care of their knees, including supervised and specialized weight training and conditioning.

COLLEGE CALL CHECKLIST

SPORTS

If you are working with a NCAA school, make sure you will follow the regulations exactly. Otherwise, you will disqualify yourself.

What is the graduation rate for athletes for your sport at this school?

Is tutoring available if necessary during the season?

Is study hall required?

What are the provisions of any athletic scholarship due to injury while playing athletics for the college?

What are the provisions of any athletic scholarship due to injury outside athletics?

What are the medical provisions for the athletes?

What are the drug testing policies?

What is your team's/school's record as far as NCAA or NAIA investigations and violations, if any?

What will cause dismissal from the team?

Is the coach's philosophy similar to what you have experienced?

What will be my athletic responsibilities to the school/team during off-season?

How many freshmen actually get to play?

Is there a freshman or junior varsity team option?

How many others are being recruited for my position?

Are the athletes house together in the dorms?

Can an athlete live off campus or belong to a fraternity or a sarority?

What are your conditioning programs?

Are stat sheets required?

What should be included?

What are your video requirements and guidelines? Is there a requirement on length?

What are your news clipping guidelines?

On-site visit by college coach to see game required, or advised?

Team try-outs available at college? (only for NCAS Div. II)

If I get hurt or end my career, will I be happy at this college?

(Continued)

What are the summer employment opportunities?

What is the practice schedule like and how long do practices run?

What are practices like?

What is the extent of travel when competing?

What are the travel conditions (room & board) when competing?

How long does it take for an athlete in your sport to graduate from this school?

What are the drug stats on your team?

What are the crime stats on your team?

What is the coaching philosophy on discipline?

What is the physical condition of the playing and training facilities, locker rooms, etc.?

For female athletes, are there specialized conditioning programs available to strengthen legs, etc. to reduce injury?

College visits

The importance of the college visit is to give you a personal view of that institution. Often a decision is based on the on-site experience or conversation with a professor. Think of the college visit similar to buying a new car and the cost of college for four years is about the same as buying a luxury sports car.

> "I have always believed that a person should not make decisions until they have accrued all of the data possible. One does not buy a house until they have visited it several times, had a termite inspection and perhaps even hired a professional home inspector to check out the entire house. We then search for the best loans, with the best rates, etc., etc.
>
> It never ceases to amaze me how many parents will send their children off to a college that they have never visited and often neither has their child. I cannot imagine sending the most precious thing in the world to me, my child, to a strange city, full of strangers without doing my own inspection, visiting and asking questions. I cannot imagine spending $100,000 dollars, which is not unusual for college these days, and not doing my homework. I would not buy a house for that sight unseen!
>
> I always advise parents and students to do their research (i.e. use the Internet, read books, talk to alumni, etc.) but always remember the importance of visiting and getting your own feel for a place before you make one of the most important decisions of your life. I do not believe there is one school that is the perfect fit, but I do believe you can get close if you do your research and visit, visit, visit!"
>
> John B., High School Counselor

> "Remember that life is a journey and the college decision process is a part of that journey. Discover what is really important to you, and then navigate through the decision process by visiting campuses. Often it is the feel you have on a campus that helps you decide what choice is right for you."
>
> Susan G., Senior High School Counselor

The college visitation process can also help eliminate schools, which may have appeared great on paper, but upon visiting, are not the best for you.

If you must visit during a special college visit day, make sure you revisit the campus. On special college visit days, you'll see the college under the best conditions.

A visit will also be a good indicator as to how you will be treated as a student at that institution. If you're not treated well on a visit...

Make appointments with each school—don't just appear—and set them up through the admissions representative you have been working with. These visits should ideally take place while school is in session so you'll have the true impression of the college. Arrange appointments with professors in departments that are in the areas of studies that are of interest to you. You'll get a chance to ask questions, meet students, eat the food, and perhaps spend the night in the dorm and attend a class or two.

A night spent in the dorms and a dorm meal can be more enlightening about the college than any tour.

Meet with someone from the Honors College/Program or the Scholarship and Financial Aid Office. These departmental face-to-face meetings may become pivotal not only in acceptance to the school, but for departmental scholarships later.

> "My biggest benefit in choosing my college was that my best friend's mom works in the Science Hall Division Office. She helped me out by setting up appointments with chemistry professors and telling me the "ins and outs" of Science Hall. Getting to talk to chemistry professors really helped me in making my final decision of becoming a chemistry major here."
>
> Lisa, student

Another advantage to on-site visiting is driving around the neighborhoods surrounding the campus. Try and drive around at night. Sometimes the information and impressions of the geographical neighborhood are more informative than the college visit itself. When you walk on campus (tour and/or by yourself) look for lighting, locked doors, access to dorms, and the number and location of emergency phones.

> "Go on several campus tours. This gives you a first-hand look at the college, plus you get out of school for a day. What more can a person ask for?"
>
> Cathe, student

Meet with college representatives when they visit your high school, though this may prove to be difficult if you have a heavy academic load.

Besides high school on-site college representative visits, universities will often have a citywide evening reception. There might also be the opportunity for an alumni visit. While all of these home city activities are helpful for information purposes, nothing can take the place of an actual visit to the college.

Summer college visiting

If you can, try and space out visits so they don't all run together in your mind later. Take notes immediately.

Keep notes on how you are treated during phone calls and especially during college visits. This will often be an indicator of how you will be treated as a student at that university.

Do your college visiting. Take all your relevant college information on that school with you on your trip. Take those notes as you go—it's very hard to reconstruct later.

TIME OUT

A virtual tour does not replace an actual visit to a campus! You need to visit. You need to walk the real sidewalks and understand how far it really is on foot between the English Hall and the Science Labs or if there's a snowstorm, how far is it really from the Residential Quad to the Lecture Hall.

Another way to enrich your information about the college that you are researching is to obtain the school's newspapers. Online you will find links to college newspapers at the College Press Network, http://www.cpnet.com

Visit information for your senior year

You can also attend the Fall Open Houses available to seniors—usually an overnight visit is included.

A post-application visit or revisit can assist in clarifying the order of preference in your mind of the final colleges on your list.

A post-acceptance visit—sometimes done at Spring Open House is similar in purpose to the post-application visit. It is the final chance for the university to sell you on that school.

PARENTS CORNER

When you visit the colleges you think are your child's top picks, while they are busy with an interview or visiting a class, go to the campus bookstore. Purchase something small, like a key chain or a car window sticker—something that has the school logo on it. When he/she makes the final decision, you can present your child with this surprise. It's fun and it let's them know you're proud of his/her choice.

Get organized!

In one year, your life will switch into high gear. Now is a good time to get yourself in the habit of staying on top of things. Trust me, in the next two years, you'll need it.

> "Traditionally the most daunting and frustrating activity a student and family sets out to accomplish is the college search. Anything that can minimize this anxious time is appreciated."
>
> Robert E. N., Chairperson,
> Pupil Personnel Services, High School

Sort the mail as it comes through the door. Say, for example, you hate Science and you get a brochure for an engineering school, throw it out immediately. Tame that Paper Monster now while he is still small. If you're not sure, don't throw away the rest of it yet. Just put it somewhere in a box or two. If you aren't at a decision point yet, then sort by regions and states.

GET ORGANIZED

Get several large boxes (bankers' boxes with the sliding drawer work well), a lot of regular file folders and some hanging file folders. Mark the hanging file folders with geographical regions or whatever criteria makes sense to you. Your aim here is to get a handle on the amount of paper. Following the example of geography, then mark the regular file folders with the states' names. Place them within the appropriate region as an example, California within the West Region hanging file folder. As the materials come in the door, put them in the appropriate file folder.

So when does this start? For some teens, it's as early as 8th and 9th grade, if they were participants in their regional academic talent searches, or were state or regionally recognized athletes or musicians. But for the rest of you (which is most of you), the avalanche of paper starts after the first college admissions test: PSAT, PLAN, ACT or SAT.

Fast forward and it's now your junior in high school. It's time to bring the hundreds of colleges down to some manageable number.

Get out the top college search parameters you worked on earlier in this section. If it's been awhile since you've worked on them, re-evaluate and make sure that they are still valid. For example, if geography isn't a criterion for you, then go through each state and pull the colleges that meet your top criteria—such as what you think your major or area of interest might be. But if geography is one of your sorting mechanisms, then pull the states that fit the criteria. Put the "active" states/schools into a separate box(es). [Again, don't throw away the schools that don't fit into your scheme—not yet—just put them in boxes by themselves. You never know what could spark your interest in the next year.

Think you're done? No way. You may have narrowed it down to a few dozen schools but the fun hasn't even begun yet. You'll need to try and narrow the vast amount of colleges down to ten or 12. How do you narrow all the schools down to just ten to 12? Based on the criteria you feel is most important to you—for example: tuition, availability of scholarships, area of study (major), urban or rural, and student population—sort through the file folders.

Another way to pare down the number of colleges and universities is by breaking them down into the three groups: (1) reach college—a school you really want to go to but may have a hard time getting into (2) reasonably attainable colleges and (3) sure-shot college (those you know you'll get into.)

Move the materials and file folders for your top ten to 15 choices into a different box from the rest. Put each school in its own file folder. On the front of the file folder, write the name of the college rep, the phone numbers, etc. This will make it easier to make phone calls and arrange college visits. Put this active box somewhere it easily can be found. [Again, don't throw the other stuff away yet. Just add the box(es) to the stack!]

Worried about narrowing your list of colleges down? Don't! With all your brainstorming, the information on your college call checklists, your conversations with college admissions reps, it will happen automatically. Arrange to visit the campuses of some of your top picks sometime during second semester or summer. As you visit each school, take the College Call Checklist. Take notes as you go. If you wait until you get home, you're bound to forget. The colleges will all start running together in your mind after awhile, especially if you visit more than one college per visit.

TIME OUT

Let your parents get involved. If they're going to be paying for college, they are entitled to know what's going on. And as your schoolwork and college search increases, the 2 extra brains, hands, etc. will help you out tremendously. They may even offer to type out your applications, make phone calls, etc.

For the final six: Get heavy duty file folders in one color, (blue for example) for the admission application, supporting documentation and application checklist for each school. Write all names and phone numbers on the blue file folder. Get another set of file folders in a different color (yellow for instance) to use for any separate scholarship applications and other scholarship material for the school. Slip this yellow scholarship folder inside the blue college application folder. Label the tabs so you can easily tell which school the folders belong to if they become separated.

Use the expanding folder for each university and keep the application and scholarship folders PLUS all documentation for that school in that expanding file.

Keep all of these active files in a box separate from the remaining other colleges.

Fill out as many applications out as possible during the summer to relieve the stress during the fall semester. And trust me, there will be stress. Remember some deadlines for scholarships (both school-based and independent) are in early fall (September/October).

For the applications that are not available during the summer, look through your accumulated documentation for prior years' applications from your final six. Or check with your guidance counselor's office for old applications. Essays may or may not change from year-to-year, but they often will be similar. Spend the summer accumulating data and practicing the essays.

Get your resume in great shape, because every application, scholarship application, and special recognition program will want a copy.

Highlights

★ The onslaught of tests begin this year, and they aren't for practice anymore either! If you don't feel confident in your scores, take a prep class to help. Remember, though, you can take them again this year and even next year, but you must start now!

★ There are all kinds of colleges out there. It's up to you to sift through the mounds of paper piling up in your room and discover your dream college. This research has to start now so, in a year's time, when you start filling out applications, you'll be one step ahead of the game!

★ Like you don't have enough lists right now? Well, this is one vital. With it, you will oh, so easily narrow down the list of schools that interest you. And you'll clean your room at the same time!

★ While we are on the topic of cutting that list of schools, why don't you visit some schools that make that cut? This will give you the real live experience of that particular school.

★ "Clean up that room!" Now, do you really want to listen to that for the next two years? The point here is to get organized and stay organized. You think your room is messy now? Wait until all those colleges are finished sending you stuff. Stay on the ball form the beginning so you avoid the nagging.

Chapter 7

The Final Countdown

- ✔ The last lap
- ✔ Interview with an admissions officer
- ✔ Put it in writing
- ✔ Down paper monster, down!
- ✔ Tying up loose ends

The last lap

Finally, it's your last year of high school. You've been waiting for this moment for a long time. The good news is that college is only one year away. The bad news is that college is only one year away. You have only a few more months to get all the most important pieces of the college admissions process prepared on time. This chapter will help you develop a schedule for the all-important senior year so that you can keep track of all the deadlines and procedures. You can get a perfect score on the SAT, but it won't count if you don't get your score in on time.

As early as possible, get the required recommendations for college applications and scholarship applications (there may be separate ones for each school.) Pick teachers who know you well and respect and like you. A recommendation written by someone who doesn't know you is often not useful. Be courteous and don't wait until the last minute. Give your teacher plenty of time to think and write. Keep in mind that the majority of deadlines fall either right before or right after the winter holiday break. The teachers you ask recommendations for are also probably being asked for recommendations from many other students. Teachers have familiy responsibilites, too and papers to grade over the holidays in addition to writing senior recommendations. Remember to give them as much information as possible.And don't forget to say thanks.

In addition to personal comments, teachers, are often asked to rate the following for each student:

- *Academic motivation*
- *Academic self-discipline*
- *Leadership*
- *Warmth of personality*
- *Personal initiative*
- *Respect accorded by faculty*

To assist teachers in writing recommendations for you, attach a copy of your resume to your request. This will help them add details to the recommendations for you.

September

- *Early in the month, find out your school's procedure for processing transcript requests, recommendations, and college and scholarship applications. You have to follow their instructions correctly so that your applications are not delayed.*
- *Meet with your guidance counselor to confirm your college choices and confirm that they are consistent with your academic history. Some colleges have deadlines during the early fall of senior year. Make sure you have time to complete the application process if a college has an early deadline.*

- *During the second week of September, the National Merit Scholarship Corporation will notify your school with the names of the semi-finalists for their scholarships. You are given a detailed application and essay which you have one to two weeks to complete. About 10 days later, the public semi-finalist announcements will be made.*
- *If you take the SAT or ACT again, do it early, so if you're still not happy with your score, you can take them again. Remember that colleges must have your score by the application deadline.*
- *Depending on the colleges you are considering, you may also need to take the SAT II subject area achievement tests. All are not offered at every test site, so be sure to check locations. Take them in the fall so your colleges will have the score by the deadline. These same colleges may also require you to take the Test of Written English (TWE). This can be taken on the same morning as one of your SAT II exams.*
- *Check and double-check admissions and scholarship deadlines.*
- *Ask teachers for recommendations now, if you haven't done so already.*

Make a master schedule of dates, deadlines, and stick them on the refrigerator in your kitchen. Then everyone in the house will know when a deadline is coming and there will be no way you can miss one.

SAMPLE MASTER COLLEGE COUNTDOWN SCHEDULE
SENIOR YEAR

May	
5/1	Pull together all of the offers and make a final decision.
April	
	Start pulling together the offers as they come in.
March	
3/15	Independent scholarship applications due.
February	
2/15–2/20	Make sure SAR is correct and reported back to colleges.
2/15 or so	receive SAR back.
January	
	FAFSA needs to be filed
1/15	College applications due
December	
	Winter Break: fill out applications due in January
12/1	College applications due
November	
11/15	College applications due
October	
10/15	Independent scholarship application due
10/1	College application due
September	
	2nd week—National Merit announces Semi-Finalists
	Attend Open Houses
	Take SAT/ACT again
	Find out school's procedure for handling applications, scholarships, etc.

October through December

Colleges will most likely have open houses at this time. If the school you are considering has one, it is important that you attend. If a merit-based scholarship is under consideration, you must attend. If you can't make it, call to schedule an appointment to go over what you missed.

TIME OUT

Be on the look out for scholarship opportunities not tied to a particular college. Get information from your guidance office, the Internet, and reference books. Many of these scholarships have their deadlines in the fall, although the awards are not announced until after your senior year is over.

In late winter, the White House Presidential Scholars will notify the first pool of candidates for their program. Entrance is based on the highest SAT and ACT scores in the country. You cannot apply. The Presidential Scholars Commission will notify you if you qualify. Keep in mind that there is an extensive application to fill out, so give yourself plenty of time.

If any of the colleges you are considering require a 7th semester transcript, make sure it is done as soon as it is available . Watch for deadlines, too.

The NMSC announces the finalists in February and the winners in April.

TIME OUT

Give your guidance counselor plenty of time to process your application. Many other students will also be asking for his help. Don't ask for assistance the day before the application is due. In some high schools, only one counselor writes all recommendations required by colleges. If this is the case in your school, make sure that counselor has adequate information about you. A copy of your resume will help. Make sure this is done very early in the year.

If you are requesting an early decision, the deadlines range from October to December. Some deadlines are as early as September and October.

Early decision is a contractual agreement between you and the college that says if you are accepted, you will withdraw all other applications and make that school your choice. This is mostly for the highly competitive schools whose freshman classes fill up very quickly. Early decision guarantees an admissions slot for you. This is great if you are certain you wish to attend that school. It gets the worry over early, but it also takes any other options out of the picture. So, if the request for an early decision was done on an impulse, and you accept, you may have a problem. The pressure is for real.

You should prepare applications and essays for other schools in case the college you requested an early decision for doesn't accept you.

Interview with an admissions officer

The interview used to be a standard requirement in almost all college admissions. Due to budget constraints, the interview is becoming less impportant in the college admissions decision.

The interview is still a requirement for the vast majority of top-flight merit based scholarships. Make sure your child schedules an interview, especially if his chance of attending a college is dependent upon financial aid.

Up until the interview, you are just a name on an application. The interview is your chance to personalize the process in the eyes of the admissions rep.

Interviewing is a two-way street. It should be more of a conversation than a question session.You need to be prepared to talk about your strengths and talents and to have done your homework about the school.

Practice your interviewing skills well in advance of your interviews. There are reference books available on college interviewing which have lists of sample questions. Practice out loud with another person taking the role of the interviewer. If necessary, ask for assistance from your high school guidance counselor. Start practicing with friends and then try and arrange practice time with an adult, preferrably not with your parents.

Spend the time necessary to make the answer to the questions truly part of you so you sound natural and don't stumble. Be an active participant in the interview. Your interview should be more like a conversation than a series of questions.

The following is a short list of typical questions covered in an interview:

- *Who you are—really?*
- *How do you like the school?*
- *What are your interests outside of academics?*
- *How do you view the world?*
- *What would you change in the world if you could?*
- *What has your high school experience been like?*
- *How would you describe yourself in three to five adjectives?*
- *Who are your favorite musicians and actors?*
- *What are your hobbies?*
- *What is special about your family?*
- *Who is your favorite author?*
- *What is the latest book you read outside of course work?*
- *Why do you want to go to college?*
- *Why do you want to go to this college?*
- *What first brought this college to your attention?*

- *What do you think your major will be?*
- *What do you want to do with your degree and your life?*
- *What have you enjoyed about this visit so far?*

You should dress nicely and cleanly; not necessary to be dressed up—just enough so the rep realizes you have made the effort to take this meeting seriously.

- *Never answer questions with just a couple of words. Complete sentences are necessary.*
- *Do not be negative about anything.*

Be on time for your college interviews, whether they are at your high school or during a campus on-site visit. If you can't make it, call and reschedule. Don't just skip without notice. Do your homework about the school and have questions ready for your interviewer.

Interviews can be on campus, in a hotel or restaurant in your city, or at your high school. They can be with admissions reps or with alumni. Take advantage of college reps' visits to your high school. Those visits can save you a trip or reconfirm your relationship with the college rep.

For your first visit and interview, try a college in your hometown. This is just like a first job interview. It's nerve racking and you just have to get it over with. This will help you get over your nervousness while giving you a standard to judge other visits and interviews.

The application essay

This is your chance to personalize your application. Make the most of it. Use your resume as the skeleton for your knowledge base about yourself. Look at yourself and pick your most important personal characteristics and write about those. Think about someone who has had an impact in your life. Most importantly, take your time.

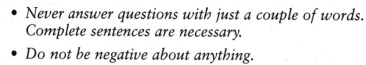

Choose a topic you feel you are comfortable with. Be honest in your writing. The admissions committees read a very large number of applications and essays each year. Try to make your writing something very close to home so that honesty will come through in your writing.

> "Write your entrance essay about what you know and what is real to you. Fabrications are easy to detect when they don't come from your heart."
>
> Cathe, student

Stay on topic and make sure you answer the question.

Take your time and think about yourself and the essay questions themselves. Do an outline or a sketch of the points you want to make. Do several drafts. If at all possible, leave some time (a day at least) between each step.

Have someone else proof your essay. No one catches all of his or her errors.

Some high schools have a committee of teachers who read all students' college and scholarship essays. Most students don't have this type of resource available to them, so you have to go and find your own readers.

Creativity and gentle humor, where appropriate, are hallmarks of the most successful essays. Your essay can be funny, slightly irreverent, but cannot have any errors in it such as bad grammar and spelling. Avoid discussing relationships, religion, sex, or your SAT/ACT score.

If there have been some special circumstances during your high school career, a personal essay is the time and place to discuss them. The essay is your chance to have your say and to give the admissions committee a chance to know you.

The Steps in Writing an Essay

Preparation
- Brainstorming
- Grouping and revision
- Focusing
- Organizing

Drafting
- Introduction
- Body
- Conclusion

Editing
Final Version

With your resume and your essays on the computer, make sure you backup your files often.

Internet sites that provide assistance on essay writing:

Writing the College Admission Essay:

http://icpae.indiana.edu/infoseries/is-15.html

Princeton Review:

http://www.review.com

Application Essay from Peterson:

http://www.petersons.com/ugrad/applications.html

Elements of Style by Columbia University

http://www.columbia.edu.acis/bartleby/strunk

Put it in writing

Never assume you will automatically be sent an application. Call early and ask when they will be mailed out. Follow-up if you don't receive one by that date. Prepare now for the number of essays for applications and scholarships from fall until spring. Ask your parents to help out by filling in information like your name and address.Take your time. Double-check everything. Type or print very neatly on the applications.

Make copies of everything.

After you have double-checked everything, do it again.

If the college you applied to has rolling admissions, you will be notified once the college has reviewed your application. Get your application in early. Some colleges with rolling admissions close their freshman class as early as October or November.

The following are examples of self-addressed, stamped post cards to be used with each request to your high school to provide you with a record of when the high school mailed applications or transcripts to the university. If something is lost along the way, these records may be useful.

EXAMPLE OF RESPONSE POST CARD FOR APPLICATION

The application information for (student's name) (university's name) at (city, state) has been sent from (high school name) on

______________________, ___________

EXAMPLE OF RESPONSE POST CARD FOR TRANSCRIPT

(student's name) (high school's name) transcript
has been mailed to (university's name) on

______________________, ___________

EXAMPLE OF RESPONSE POST CARD FOR RECOMMENDATION

The recommendation for (student's name) was sent
to (university's name) on

______________________, ___________

Signed ______________________________

The following pages contain a sample copy of the Common Application. The Common Application is a product of the National Association of Secondary School Principals (NASSP) It is an attempt to keep the application workload down for college-bound seniors by providing a single application that can be sent to several colleges. At this time, almost 200 U.S. colleges use the Common Application. [A paper copy is available from your guidance counselor or the NASSP at 1904 Association Drive, Reston, VA 20191-1537.]

We're using the Common Application to show what a typical college application looks like. There is a section which asks for information such as your name, social security number, address, phone number, where you go to high school and when you expect to graduate.

Another section may ask if your parents, grandparents, or other relatives went to the college and when they graduated.

Another section of a college application may ask for what classes in the core subject areas you have taken so far and what courses you are presently taking (and are going to take) as a senior. It may or may not ask for you to put down your grades. In most cases, it will ask if the courses were honors or AP/IB.

Another section of a college application is asking for you to list activities, honors, etc. This is where your resume that is discussed in the 9th grade chapter comes into play. If you have been keeping your resume up-to-date, all you have to do is rearrange it in the order that matches the college application form, print it out, and staple it to the application. In the boxes, type or neatly print, "see attached."

Another section of the application might be the short essay questions—where there will be a series of questions where the answers are one to five sentences long.

Another section of the application might be the traditional essay question(s). [For hints about essay writing, etc., see earlier in this chapter for a discussion on college application essay writing.] Most of the time, the essay is word processed and then attached to the application proper. Make sure that you put the name of the college, your name, your social security number, and the year of admission on the top of the essay in case your essay gets separated from the rest of the application.

A section of the application will cover information that can only be filled out by your guidance counseling office. You will submit your application to the office once everything is completed along with your check or money order as the application fee.

There may be a section built directly into the application for counselor or teacher recommendation(s). If so, you will need to submit the application form to the guidance office or your teacher for recommendations eith the instructions to forward it to the guidance office. Most of the time, the teacher recommendations are considered to be separate documents to be included in the package that gets sent to the college with the application.

Some colleges would prefer everything to arrive in one traditional package so that everything stays together. You need to verify how the Admissions Departments of your top choices want submissions. You will also need to follow the guidelines and preferences given by your high school guidance counseling office.

As we learned above, the Common Application is used by almost 200 U.S. colleges. A list of colleges participating in the Common Application can be found at the web site http://apply.collegeEdge.com/. The National Association of Secondary School Principals (NASSP) sponsors the Common Application and each year's new version can be downloaded in August from the web site, http://nassp.org/.

You will need the software, Adobe Acrobat Reader, to access the Common Application files you have downloaded to your computer. Adobe Acrobat Reader is a free download from Adobe at http://www.adobe.com.

Applying to college—your online options

You can actually apply online to some schools. Yea for the internet!. You still need to send test scores, transcripts, recommendations, and any fees by mail, but the online application can be sent by e-mail. There will be a form on screen for you to fill out. Make sure to go over the screen application very carefully (yes, spelling too), print a copy for your records, and once everything has been double-checked, take a deep breath and hit the send button.

The college won't process your application until it receives your application fee and anything else that has to go by mail.

Web sites that offer online applications are:
Collegelink Apply! http://www.collegelink.com
CollegeNET http://www.collegenet.com/aw
Peterson's list with links to hundreds of schools' Web pages online applications http://www.petersons.com/

Two-thirds of the approximately 1,500 four-year colleges have applications online.

Adelphi • Agnes Scott • Albertson • Albion • Albright • Alfred • Allegheny • American • Amherst • Antioch • Assumption • Babson • Bard • Barnard • Bates • Beaver • Beloit • Bennington • Bentley • Birmingham-Southern Boston College • Boston University • Bowdoin • Brandeis • Bryant • Bryn Mawr • Bucknell • Butler • Carleton • Case Western Reserve • Centenary • Centre • Claremont McKenna • Clark University • Coe Colby • Colby-Sawyer • Colgate • Colorado College • Connecticut College • Cornell College • University of Dallas • Dartmouth • Davidson • Denison • University of Denver • DePauw • Dickinson • Drew • Duke Earlham • Eckerd • Elizabethtown • Elmira • Embry-Riddle • Emory • Eugene Lang • Fairfield • Fisk • Fordham • Franklin & Marshall • Furman • George Washington • Gettysburg • Gonzaga Goucher • Grinnell • Guilford • Gustavus Adolphus • Hamilton Harvard-Radcliffe • Harvey Mudd • Haverford • Hendrix Holy Cross • Hood • Ithaca • Johns Hopkins • Juniata Lawrence • Le Moyne • Lehigh • Lewis & Clark • Linfield Macalester • Manhattan • Manhattanville • Marietta Millsaps • Moravian • Morehouse • Mount Holyoke Ohio Wesleyan • University of the Pacific • Pitzer • Pomona Randolph-Macon Woman's • Redlands • Reed • Regis College

COMMON APPLICATION©
1999 – 2000

Hampden-Sydney • Hampshire • Hanover • Hartwick Hiram • Hobart & William Smith • Hofstra • Hollins Kalamazoo • Kenyon • Knox • Lafayette • Lake Forest Loyola College • Loyola University (La.) • Lynchburg Marquette • University of Miami • Middlebury • Mills Muhlenberg • New York University • Oberlin • Occidental University of Portland • Puget Sound • Randolph-Macon Regis University • Rensselaer • Rhodes • Rice • University of Richmond

Ripon • Rochester Institute of Technology • University of Rochester • Roger Williams • Rollins • St. Benedict & St. John's • St. Joseph's University • St. Lawrence • St. Louis University • St. Michael's • St. Norbert • St. Olaf Salem • Santa Clara • Sarah Lawrence • Scranton • Scripps • Seattle University • Simmons • Skidmore • Smith • University of the South • Southern Methodist • Southwestern • Spelman • Stetson • Stonehill • Suffolk • Susquehanna Swarthmore • Syracuse • TCU • Trinity College (Conn.) • Trinity University • Tufts • Tulane • Tulsa • Union • Ursinus • Utica • Valparaiso • Vanderbilt • Vassar • Wabash • Wagner • Wake Forest • Washington College Washington University • Washington & Lee • Wellesley • Wells • Wesleyan • Western Maryland • Westminster (Pa.) • Wheaton • Whitman • Whittier • Widener • Willamette • Williams • Wittenberg • Wooster • WPI

APPLICATION FOR UNDERGRADUATE ADMISSION

The colleges and universities listed above encourage the use of this application. No distinction will be made between it and the college's own form. The accompanying instructions tell you how to complete, copy, and file your application with any one or several of the colleges. Please type or print in black ink.

PERSONAL DATA

Legal name: ____ ____________
Last/Family *First* *Middle (complete)* *Jr., etc.* *Gender*

Prefer to be called: ____________________ (nickname) Former last name(s) if any: ____________________

Are you applying as a ☐ freshman or ☐ transfer student? For the term beginning: ____________________

Permanent home address: ____
Number and Street

____
City or Town *State* *Country* *Zip Code + 4 or Postal Code*

If different from the above, please give your mailing address for all admission correspondence:

Mailing address: (use from ________ to ________) ______________________________
(Dates) *Number and Street*

____
City or Town *State* *Country* *Zip Code + 4 or Postal Code*

Phone at mailing address: (__________) ______________ Permanent home phone: (__________) ______________
Area Code *Number* *Area Code* *Number*

E-mail address: ____

Birthdate: ____________________ Citizenship: ☐ U.S./dual U.S. citizen. If dual, specify other citizenship: ____________________

☐ U.S. Permanent Resident visa. Citizen of ____________________. ☐ Other citizenship: ______________ / ______________
Country *Visa Type*

If you are not a U.S. citizen and live in the United States, how long have you been in the country? ____________________

Possible area(s) of academic concentration/major: ______________________________ or undecided ☐

Special college or division if applicable: ______________________________

Possible career or professional plans: ______________________________ or undecided ☐

Will you be a candidate for financial aid? ☐ Yes ☐ No If yes, the appropriate form(s) was/will be filed on: ______________

The following items are optional: Social Security number, if any: ___ ___ ___ - ___ ___ - ___ ___ ___ ___

Place of birth: ______________________________ Marital status: ______________
City *State* *Country*

First language, if other than English: ____________________ Language spoken at home: ____________________

If you wish to be identified with a particular ethnic group, please check the following:

☐ African American, Black
☐ American Indian, Alaskan Native (tribal affiliation ______________ enrolled ______)
☐ Asian American (country of family's origin ____________________)
☐ Asia (Indian Subcontinent) (country ____________________)
☐ Hispanic, Latino (country ____________________)
☐ Mexican American, Chicano
☐ Native Hawaiian, Pacific Islander
☐ Puerto Rican
☐ White or Caucasian
☐ Other (Specify ____________________)

EDUCATIONAL DATA

School you now attend: ______________________ Date of entry: ______________

Address: ______________________ CEEB/ACT code: ______________

City or Town *State* *Country* *Zip Code + 4 or Postal Code*

Date of secondary graduation: ____________ Is your school public? ______ private? ______ parochial? ______

College counselor: Name: ______________________ Position: ______________

Counselor's phone: (________) ______________ Counselor's FAX: (________) ______________

Area Code *Number* *Ext.* *Area Code* *Number*

List all other secondary schools, including summer schools and programs you have attended beginning with ninth grade.

Name of School — Location (City, State, Zip) — Dates Attended

____

____

List all colleges at which you have taken courses for credit and list names of courses taken and grades earned on a separate sheet. Please have an official transcript sent from each institution as soon as possible.

Name of College — Location (City, State, Zip) — Degree Candidate? — Dates Attended

____

____

If not currently attending school, please check here: ☐ Describe in detail, on a separate sheet, your activities since last enrolled.

TEST INFORMATION. Be sure to note the tests required for each institution to which you are applying. The official scores from the appropriate testing agency must be submitted to each institution as soon as possible. Please list your test plans below.

ACT

Date Taken/ To Be Taken	*English Score*	*Math Score*	*Reading Score*	*Science Score*	*Composite Score*
Date Taken	*English Score*	*Math Score*	*Reading Score*	*Science Score*	*Composite Score*

SAT I

Date Taken/ To Be Taken	*Verbal Score*	*Math Score*	*Date*	*Verbal Score*	*Math Score*

SAT II Subject Tests

Date	*Subject*	*Score*	*Date*	*Subject*	*Score*	*Date*	*Subject*	*Score*
Date	*Subject*	*Score*	*Date*	*Subject*	*Score*	*Date*	*Subject*	*Score*

Test of English as a Foreign Language (TOEFL)

Date Taken/ To Be Taken	*Score*	*Date*	*Score*

FAMILY

Mother's full name: ______________________ Father's full name: ______________________

Is she living? ______________________ Is he living? ______________________

Home address if different from yours: ______________________ Home address if different from yours: ______________________

Occupation: ______________________ *(Describe briefly)* Occupation: ______________________ *(Describe briefly)*

Name of business or organization: ____________ Name of business or organization: ____________

College (if any): ____________ College (if any): ____________

Degree: ____________ Year: ______ Degree: ____________ Year: ______

Professional or graduate school (if any): ____________ Professional or graduate school (if any): ____________

Degree: ____________ Year: ______ Degree: ____________ Year: ______

If not with both parents, with whom do you make your permanent home? ______________________

Please check if parents are ☐ married ☐ separated ☐ divorced (date____________) ☐ other ____________

Please give names and ages of your brothers or sisters. If they have attended college, give the names of the institutions attended, degrees, and approximate dates: ______________________

____

Adelphi • Agnes Scott • Albertson • Albion • Albright • Alfred • Allegheny • American • Amherst • Antioch • Assumption • Babson • Bard • Barnard • Bates • Beaver • Beloit • Bennington • Bentley • Birmingham-Southern Boston College • Boston University • Bowdoin • Brandeis • Bryant • Bryn Mawr • Bucknell • Butler • Carleton • Case Western Reserve • Centenary • Centre • Claremont McKenna • Clark University • Coe Colby • Colby-Sawyer • Colgate • Colorado College • Connecticut College • Cornell College • University of Dallas • Dartmouth • Davidson • Denison • University of Denver • DePauw • Dickinson • Drew • Duke Earlham • Eckerd • Elizabethtown • Elmira • Embry-Riddle • Emory • Eugene Lang • Fairfield • Fisk • Fordham • Franklin & Marshall • Furman • George Washington • Gettysburg • Gonzaga Goucher • Grinnell • Guilford • Gustavus Adolphus • Hamilton Hampden-Sydney • Hampshire • Hanover • Hartwick Harvard-Radcliffe • Harvey Mudd • Haverford • Hendrix Hiram • Hobart & William Smith • Hofstra • Hollins Holy Cross • Hood • Ithaca • Johns Hopkins • Juniata Kalamazoo • Kenyon • Knox • Lafayette • Lake Forest Lawrence • Le Moyne • Lehigh • Lewis & Clark • Linfield Loyola College • Loyola University (La.) • Lynchburg Macalester • Manhattan • Manhattanville • Marietta Marquette • University of Miami • Middlebury • Mills Millsaps • Moravian • Morehouse • Mount Holyoke Muhlenberg • New York University • Oberlin • Occidental Ohio Wesleyan • University of the Pacific • Pitzer • Pomona University of Portland • Puget Sound • Randolph-Macon Randolph-Macon Woman's • Redlands • Reed • Regis College Regis University • Rensselaer • Rhodes • Rice • University of Richmond Ripon • Rochester Institute of Technology • University of Rochester • Roger Williams • Rollins • St. Benedict & St. John's • St. Joseph's University • St. Lawrence • St. Louis University • St. Michael's • St. Norbert • St. Olaf Salem • Santa Clara • Sarah Lawrence • Scranton • Scripps • Seattle University • Simmons • Skidmore • Smith • University of the South • Southern Methodist • Southwestern • Spelman • Stetson • Stonehill • Suffolk • Susquehanna Swarthmore • Syracuse • TCU • Trinity College (Conn.) • Trinity University • Tufts • Tulane • Tulsa • Union • Ursinus • Utica • Valparaiso • Vanderbilt • Vassar • Wabash • Wagner • Wake Forest • Washington College Washington University • Washington & Lee • Wellesley • Wells • Wesleyan • Western Maryland • Westminster (Pa.) • Wheaton • Whitman • Whittier • Widener • Willamette • Williams • Wittenberg • Wooster • WPI

SCHOOL REPORT

SECONDARY SCHOOL COUNSELOR EVALUATION

The colleges and universities listed above encourage the use of this form. No distinction will be made between it and the college's own form. The accompanying instructions tell you how to complete, copy, and file your application with any one or several of the colleges. Please type or print in black ink.

TO THE APPLICANT:

After filling in the information below, give this form to your college counselor. Social Security No.: ______________ *(Optional)*

Student name: ______________________________
Last/Family *First* *Middle (complete)* *Jr., etc.*

Address: ______________________________
Number and Street *City or Town* *State* *Country* *Zip Code + 4 or Postal Code*

Current year courses—please indicate title, level (AP, IB, advanced, honors, etc.) and credit value of all courses you are taking this year.

First Semester/Trimester:	Second Semester/Trimester:	Third Trimester:
____________	____________	____________
____________	____________	____________
____________	____________	____________
____________	____________	____________
____________	____________	____________
____________	____________	____________
____________	____________	____________

TO THE SECONDARY SCHOOL COLLEGE COUNSELOR: **Attach applicant's official transcript, including courses in progress, a school profile, and transcript legend. (Please check transcript copies for readability.) After filling in the blanks below, use both sides of this form to describe the applicant. Please provide all available information for this candidate:**

H.S. graduation date: ____________

Class rank: ________ in a class of ________ , covering a period from ________ *(mo./yr.)* to ________ *(mo./yr.)*.

The rank is ☐ *weighted* ☐ *unweighted* How many students share this rank? ____________

If a precise rank is not available, please indicate rank to the nearest tenth from the top. ____________

Cumulative GPA: ________ on a ________ scale, covering a period from ________ *(mo./yr.)* to ________ *(mo./yr.)*.

This GPA is ☐ *weighted* ☐ *unweighted* Percentage of graduating class attending: four year: ______ two-year: ______ institutions.

In comparison to other college preparatory students *at our school,* the applicant's course selection is:

☐ most demanding ☐ very demanding ☐ demanding ☐ average ☐ less than demanding.

Are courses taken on a block schedule? ☐ Yes ☐ No If yes, in what year did block scheduling begin? ____________

Counselor's name (please print or type): ____________ ____________ *Signature*

Position: ____________ School: ____________

Counselor's address: ____________ Date: ____________

Counselor's phone: (________) ____________ *Area Code* *Number* *Ext.* Counselor's FAX: (________) ____________ *Area Code* *Number*

High School CEEB/ACT Code: __ __ __ __ __ __ Counselor's e-mail: ____________

1999–2000 (See reverse side) **SR-1**

Please feel free to write whatever you think is important about this student, including a description of academic and personal characteristics. We are particularly interested in the candidate's intellectual promise, motivation, relative maturity, integrity, independence, originality, initiative, leadership potential, capacity for growth, special talents, and enthusiasm. We welcome information that will help us to differentiate this student from others.

How long have you known the applicant, and in what context? ______________________

What are the first words that come to your mind to describe the applicant? ______________________

____

Ratings (optional):

Compared to other students in his or her entire secondary school class, how do you rate this student in terms of:

No basis		Below Average	Average	Good (above average)	Very Good (well above average)	Excellent (top 10%)	One of the top few encountered in my career
	Academic Achievement						
	Extracurricular Accomplishments						
	Personal Qualities and Character						
	Creativity						

I recommend this student: ☐ With reservation ☐ Fairly strongly ☐ Strongly ☐ Enthusiastically

CONFIDENTIALITY:

We value your comments highly and ask that you complete this form in the knowledge that it may be retained in the student's file should the applicant matriculate at a member college. In accordance with the Family Educational Rights and Privacy Act of 1974, matriculating students do have access to their permanent files which may include forms such as this one. Colleges do not provide access to admissions records to applicants, those students who are denied admission, or those students who decline an offer of admission. Again, your comments are important to us and we thank you for your cooperation. These colleges are committed to administer all educational policies and activities without discrimination on the basis of race, color, religion, national or ethnic origin, age, handicap, or sex. The admissions process at private undergraduate institutions is exempt from the federal regulation implementing Title IX of the Education Amendments of 1972.

SR-2 **1999–2000**

Down paper monster, down!

This is not the time to lose anything. You have to keep your colleges files in order. Each time you speak with an admissions rep, make a note of it and put it in the file for that school.

Make copies of everything. You never know when you'll need them to replace ones that were lost, or to substantiate check numbers or dates.

TIME OUT

If you are applying for independent scholarships, start a new expanding file folder for them. File this large file folder in the box with your final schools' folders. Each independent scholarship application, checklist and supporting documentation should be in its own file folder which will be placed in the expanding file folder.

Carefully check each application package before you take it to your high school for any counseling recommendations and/or high school transcript. And then have someone else read it.

Make sure that your copy of the application package is assembled in exactly the same order that the original is in. Use a paperclip to keep it separate from the other supporting documentation in the file. Then re-file your copy in the appropriate application folder.

As you receive feedback and information from colleges, make sure you make the appropriate notations on the Application & Scholarship Checklists. (See sample starting on page 186.)

After you make your final decision; make sure you return your acceptance letter before the deadline. Usually it is May 1st, but some colleges have other deadlines. Admissions and housing deposits are usually required at this time. Make the notations on your checklist.

Send letters declining admissions and scholarship offers to the other schools and say thank you.

Make sure you send all the acceptance paperwork necessary for your scholarships by the response deadlines. This is for both scholarships from your school and for independent scholarships.

For the school you accepted, save the files. You and your parents will be adding to these files for the next several years.

For the other schools to which you were accepted, but declined, pack the files in a box and put it away where it can be found easily—just in case you change your mind.

Once you are in college, paperwork doesn't stop. Make sure you keep your paperwork on loans and scholarships current. Send important paperwork home.

An Application & Scholarship Checklist keeps the paper trail going smoothly. A separate checklist should be filled out for every application filed and for every scholarship applied for. Anytime you perform an activity for an application, mark it on the checklist with a checkmark and a date.

File the checklist and any additional paperwork in the appropriate university folder. If you have an application for a college scholarship, file that file folder inside the college application folder.

APPLICATION & SCHOLARSHIP CHECKLIST

UNIVERSITY: ______________________

DEADLINE: ______________________

APPLICATION:

- Paper application
  - Typed ______________________
  - Dated and signed ______________________
- e-mail application
  - Filled in ______________________
  - Proofed ______________________
  - Submitted via e-mail ______________________
  - Admissions fee check mailed ______________________
- On-line application form
  - Filled in ______________________
  - Printed ______________________
  - Dated and signed ______________________

RESUME:

- Updated ______________________
- In their format
  - Typed/printed on application ______________________
  - (Or) on Separate Sheets ______________________

TRANSCRIPTS:

- High School
  - Requested with stamped response card ______________________
  - Response card received ______________________
- Other College Attended
  - Copy Made of Request & Check ______________________
  - Requested ______________________
  - Mailed, per their confirmation ______________________

TESTS TAKEN

- ACT
  - Registration Mailed ______________________

(Continued)

Test Taken, Date ______

Scores Received ______

SAT

Registration Mailed ______

Test Taken, Date ______

Scores Received ______

SAT II (ACHIEVEMENT)

Which Subjects? ______

______

______

Registration Mailed ______

Test Taken, Date ______

Scores Received ______

TWE

Registration Mailed ______

Test Taken, Date ______

Scores Received ______

TOEFL

Registration Mailed ______

Test Taken, Date ______

Scores Received ______

TEST SCORES REQUESTED TO BE SENT TO UNIVERSITY

ACT ______

SAT ______

SAT II (Achievement subject area) ______

AP/IB ______

TWE ______

TOEFL ______

SEPARATE HIGH SCHOOL RECORD FORM

Typed ______

Copy Made ______

Delivered to Appropriate

(Continued)

High School Personnel

w/Instructions and with
Stamped Response Card ________________

Response Card Received ________________

LETTERS OF RECOMMENDATION

Number Needed ________________

Requested from: ________________

____

____

____

Request Form ________________

To Whom? ________________

Typed/printed? ________________

Copy of Form Made ________________

Envelope Typed and Stamped ________________

Copy of resume attached ________________

Note w/ Instructions and deadline ________________

Delivered w/ stamped Response Card ________________

Response Card Received ________________

Thank You Note ________________

ESSAYS

How Many? ________________

Rough Draft ________________

Second Draft ________________

Word Processed or Typed on Form ________________

Proofed by someone else ________________

PERFORMING ARTS—Auditions

Solo, monologue literature obtained? ________________

Live or on tape ________________

Local/regional or on-campus ________________

Scheduled? ________________

Confirmed? ________________

(Continued)

Accompanist or tape? ______

Specialized references? ______

Clothing, equipment, props ______

Photo (if needed) taken and received? ______

VISUAL ARTS

Portfolio slides taken? ______

Portfolio slides developed? ______

Portfolio slides appropriately identified? ______

List of portfolio slides ______

Sketchbook updated? ______

Self-addressed stamped return envelop ______

Stamped response card enclosed? ______

Response card received? ______

Portfolio interview required? ______

SPORTS

Registered with NCAA Clearinghouse ______

Coach contact? ______

Letter and Video sent/ ______

Official visit? ______

Letter of Intent signing dates ______

Copy made? ______

Presented or sent ______

ADDITIONAL REQUIREMENTS BY UNIVERSITY:

SUPPLEMENTARY INFORMATION TO BE INCLUDED:

APPLICATION PACKAGE COMPLETED

(Continued)

Application Fee Check Written ______

Go Over Checklist and Application Booklet ______

Copies Made ______

FINAL PROCESSING

If High School Reporting Required ______

Directly on Application: ______

Submitted to High School w/ stamped Response Card ______

Response Card Received ______

If Mailed Directly By Student

Would w/ stamped Response Card ______

Response Card Received ______

Approximately Two Weeks Later ______

Call Admissions Rep and Verify All ______

Has Arrived And If There Is Anything Missing ______

FINANCIAL AID INFORMATION

Deadline ______

College's Own Form Required

Information Gathered? ______

Typed or Neatly Printed ______

Attachments Compiled ______

Copies Made ______

FAFSA

Form Received From Guidance Office ______

Information Gathered ______

Typed or Neatly Printed ______

Attachments? ______

Copies Made ______

SAR Report Received ______

FAF/Profile

Form Received From Guidance Office ______

Information Gathered ______

(Continued)

Typed or Neatly Printed	____________
Attachments?	____________
Copies Made	____________
Date Expected For Admission Notification	____________
Date Expected For Fancial Aid Notification	____________
Date Expected For Scholarship Notification	____________
8th Semester Grade Report Sent to University	____________
Admission Acceptance Letter Returned	____________
Admission Deposit attached	____________
Housing Deposit attached	____________
Scholarship Award Acceptance Returned	____________
Thank you letter sent for Scholarship	____________
Declining Acceptance Letter sent	____________
Declining Scholarship Letter sent	
With thank you	____________

Tying up loose ends

It may help to re-visit some of the colleges you applied to once you have applied to them. With all of the stress out of the way, you'll be able to focus on the school. It will also help you decide what school you really want to be accepted to and maybe even what school you don't want to be accepted to.

Your aid awards or award letters will be with your letters of acceptance. If you have any questions at all on these, contact each college's financial aid office for clarification. If you are concerned that the award will not sufficiently cover your needs, again speak with the college financial aid officer and request further assistance.

You are not required to accept everything on the award letter. They may have listed loans that you have realized you don't need to complete your first year. You should make those notations on the award letter.

To evaluate your awards, you will need to take into account some priority system of how the college meets your educational needs and then the financial details. You need to look at the bottom line of each award and then make a decision based on your educational needs and the amount of money you and your family can afford.

Most universities send out their decision letters from February through April. If a university has rolling admissions, then you will be notified of their decision as soon as the university has reviewed your application. Financial aid and/or scholarship information may come simultaneously or some time after the acceptance letter is sent to the student.

Once your letters of acceptance are received, consider sending in housing deposits to your top three choices. This theoretically ensures you a place in the dorms. Once your final college choice has been made and you have notified all of the universities, your other housing deposits will be refunded (less a handling charge). See the housing bulletins of each school for details.

In April, visit any colleges you have been accepted to where you need that first or second look.

Acceptance

In March and April make your final evaluations of the admissions letters and financial aid and scholarship offers. Make your decision. Your decision must be made and proper notifications made no later than May 1st, unless otherwise stated by the university. You will also need to notify the schools to which you are not accepting their offers.

Make sure you have your application for loan programs filed as soon as possible after making your school decision. At some schools, they are using the Direct Student Loan program instead of loans which are acquired directly through banking institutions.

Let your guidance counselor know which schools have accepted you, which scholarships you have been offered, and finally what your final decision is.

After all senior awards are announced, update your resume one last time.

PARENTS CORNER

Your child is not required to accept everything on the Award Letter. There may be a list of a full complement of loans that your child doesn't need to complete his/her first year. Make the proper notations on the letter.

To evaluate your awards, lay them all out on the table. You will need to take into account some priority system of how the college meets your educational needs and then the financial nuts and bolts. You need to look at the bottom line of each award and then make a decision based on your educational needs and the amount you and your family can afford.

Give thanks

If you have received specific scholarships, send thank-you notes Send a thank you note to anyone who helped you with this process.

SAMPLE OF THANK YOU FOR RECOMMENDATIONS

Date

Mrs. ______________________

High School

Dear Mrs. ______________________:

Thank you very much for writing the recommendations for me for my college admissions applications. They really helped.

Sincerely,

____

SAMPLE OF THANK YOU FOR SCHOLARSHIP

Date

Dr. ______________________

College

Dear Dr. ______________________:

Thank you very much for the scholarship award your committee gave me. My major is International Business and as you know ________________ University has one of the top International Business programs in the country. Your scholarship will assist my attendance at ________________ University.

Thanks again,

Highlights

★ Practice before you go on an interview. This is the only chance you will get to show PleaseAcceptMe U. that you're not just a name on a piece of paper.

★ Make sure your application is perfect before you send it out. Don't for get to include anything, whether it's your processing fee or a teacher recommendation.

★ Keep things organized and throw out what you no longer need. Don't miss any deadlines—use the Application & Scholarship Checklist to stay on track.

★ You need to keep checking on rolling admissions, scholarship updates, and thank you notes.

Chapter 8

Planning Ahead When You Have Special Concerns

This chapter addresses specific issues such as a physical disability that might make the journey through secondary education to college more challenging. These concerns not viewed as negatives, but they need to be acknowledged so that you know the right questions to ask during your college search. You'll find a sampling of the questions in the pages that follow that you should ask a college admissions officer when applying. Please note that the lists of questions are not complete. You will undoubtedly have more questions, depending on your condition. However, use these checklists to get you to start thinking about the type of information you will need to obtain. Also, use the checklists with the general College Call Checklists in chapter six.

A disability, at the very least, means life for you is not like it is for the majority of the world.You want to go to college. A disability is a difference. However, it is you that determines your degree of success in college and in life.

> Although affirmative action procedures should help students who are disabled, tell the admissions committees about your other activities and accomplishments. Colleges are not going to accept you solely because you increase their pool of diversity. Also, your disability is not your only characteristic. Flaunt all of your talents!
>
> Pauline, student

Testing accommodations

To make special arrangements for tests, you will need to complete a student eligibility form (obtained from your high school guidance counselor) and provide current (within the last three years) documentation with your application. You must also provide documentation that you receive specialized services or testing situations in your current school.

Registration and arrangement for these accommodations have to be set up well in advance. You are required to meet the same registration deadlines as other students. Because of the additional eligibility form, you cannot register for tests online or by FAX.

Each testing service has special disability departments that handle these issues. Your high school guidance counseling office will handle these contacts for you. You need to follow through with your counselor to make sure the contacts were made and that you know exactly what is expected of you.

Examples of accommodations are wheelchair access, a sign language interpreter for spoken instructions, extended testing time, additional breaks, a scribe to record answers, a reader to dictate test questions, and other aids used in your daily life. Examples of alternate test formats are Braille, large print, large print answer sheets, an audio cassette with a large-print figure supplement, and an audio cassette with Braille figure supplement.

COLLEGE CALL CHECKLIST

<u>If you suffer from a general physical disability, here are the types of questions you should ask:</u>

What is the department or office to assist students with disabilities?
Are there support groups available on campus?
Is the campus truly handicapped accessible?
When you visit the campus, can you get from the commonly used buildings within the time normally allotted between classes?
Are dorms truly serviceable for someone in a wheelchair?
Are classrooms for courses you will take in buildings that are fully accessible, not only into first floor doorways, but have methods to realistically reach upper floors?
Are labs adaptable to limitations,
- For example, are lab tables available for wheel chair width and height?

Are the dorms wired to support any equipment you use?

If you use a Support Dog, what are the provisions for your dog on campus and in the dorms?

What type of documentation is needed for admission with accommodations made for your physical disability?

Is there a special application required for admission due to physical disability?

Note takers available?
Alternative test situation allowed for admissions tests?
Are accommodations made for tests and exams as a student on campus?
- Individually proctored?
- Untimed or extended time?
- Reader available
- Scribe available
- Computer available

Are there waivers for courses for degree requirements?

Transportation issues on campus?
- Are on-campus student transportation vans/buses wheel chair accessible?
- Is off-campus transportation normally used by students:
  - Wheel chair accessible?
  - Regularly available?

MEDICAL SUPPORT ISSUES:

If there are heart, asthma or lung-function problems, what services are available on campus for emergency care?
When are medical support staff available on campus?
What days and hours?

(Continued)

How long does it take to get into the Student Health Center for a non-life threatening illness?

Do they accept walk-ins?

Or appointment only?

Are the specially trained personnel available in the dorms to assist in medical situations when the health center is closed?

How far is the closest hospital with a full-service emergency room?

What are the policies about attendance, official extensions and support for a student who becomes ill or suffers from a life-threatening illness?

If a student needs to take an extended leave due to illnesses, how long is allowed before the student is dropped from the university?

If you have a temporary disability, *such as a broken arm, you need to register for a later test date. If that is not possible, due to a college application deadline, ask your counselor to contact the disability department of the appropriate testing office to see what accommodations can be made to meet your needs.*

If there is an option for a personal statement essay on the essay portions of your applications, it is to your benefit to fill this out. This personal statement will allow you to share what your life is like and how you have made progress with the admissions or financial aid department.

For a teen with a disability, a campus visit becomes imperative to meet with the people who will be your advocates and mentors.

Blind or visually impaired

If you are blind or visually impaired and in high school, you have already mastered some of the skills that you will need for college.The most important skill is determination. You've had classes in orientation and mobility, life skills, social interaction skills, and safety issues. You've been exposed to instruction in academic skills in and out of the classroom that compensate for your visual disability. You will have additional questions about safety and technology.

COLLEGE CALL CHECKLIST

Are textbooks available in Braille?

Are textbooks available on tape?

Is supplementary required reading materials available in Braille?

Is supplementary required reading materials available on tape?

Are readers available?

Are audio description capabilities available for any visuals used or required for courses?

Are Optical Character Recognition (OCR) Systems available?

Are computers with voice recognition software programs vailable?

Are synthetic speech systems and/or voice synthesizer systems available?

Are magnification programs for computer screens available?

What provisions can be made for the Seeing Eye dogs that students use?

Are students available to assist a visually impaired student get across campus?

How many other blind students or visually impaired students are there on your campus?

When on your campus visit:

- Ask if it is possible to meet with a present student with visual impairments similar to you.
- Go to some classes.
- Meet with support personnel.
- When you visit the campus, walk across campus to determine if you can get from the most common buildings in the time allotted between classes.

What are the accommodations allowed for tests and exams while a student is in college, if required?

- Individually proctored?
- Untimed or extended time?
- Reader available?
- Scribe available?
- Braille test version available?
- Braille answer sheet available?
- Computer with OCR and voice synthesizer available?

Deaf or hearing impaired

Deafness is an invisible disability. But as with all disabilities, it is your positive attitude, drive and determination that will make the difference in your success in the world. Smaller sized classes will probably work the best in college for the hearing impaired, especially in discussion based courses. A small class will also make it easier to ask someone to repeat a question or a comment.

It is also important to educate your roommate about your disability. In case of a fire, for example, your roommate will need to understand that you won't be able to hear a fire alarm. Someone will have to wake you up.

> Even though a college may provide you with some equipment, acquire back-up devices if you can afford to. For example, if you stay in a different dormitory alone for whatever reason (such as during Thanksgiving holidays, etc.) you might want to have a spare smoke alarm and a TDD. Or request that the college put one in your dormitory room. Always have an extra set of hearing aids or cochlear implant devices and the accompanying equipment and then make sure you take them with you on trips. You never know when something might happen.
>
> Pauline, student

COLLEGE CALL CHECKLIST

Are signers/interpreters available?

Will student have the same interpreter?

Do you have a formal interpretation program?

- How long has your interpretation program been in place?
- How many students have used these services?

Are note takers available?

Is there a specialized interview required for disability admission?

Is there an additional application for admission with disability?

What are the accommodations allowed for tests and exams while a student is in college, if required?

- Individually proctored?
- Untimed or extended time?
- Signer available for spoken portions of tests?

Is closed caption capabilities available?

How many other deaf or hearing impaired students are there on your campus?

Is there a support group on campus?

What is the facullty attitude toward helping hearing impaired students, especially freshmen?

Will there be a specialized smoke detector in the dorm room?

Will there be a TDD in your dorm room?

When on your campus visit:

- Ask if it is possible to meet with a present student with hearing impairments similar to you.
- Go to some classes.
- Meet with support personnel.
- When you visit the campus, walk across campus to determine if you can get from the most common buildings in the time allotted between classes.

Attention Deficit/Hyperactivity Disorder (AD/HD) and/or Learning Disabled (LD)

Attention Deficit/Hyperactivity Disorder (AD/HD) and Learning Disabled (LD) are separate disabilities. However, the questions that need to be asked are very similar. You will have to use the information you know about yourself to fill in the details of your own needs and capabilities.

There are college search books for learning disabled teens. For these search books, AD/HD services are covered under the title of learning disabled (even though your child may not have any LD problems). These books rate colleges on how receptive they are to assisting teens with AD/HD.

PARENTS CORNER

Labels are often difficult to deal with. They are so difficult, that a label might keep a family from seeking help. Obtaining the appropriate support personnel and strategies for your teen depends upon documentation and an official diagnosis. There is no stigma to AD/HD or LD. AD/HD or LD is not due to a parental or moral deficiency. It is just a condition that exists in your child. Seeking help will enable your teen to obtain what he needs to fulfil his potential. With this assistance and support, kids learn coping skills that allow them to succeed. There are careers that can be matched to your teen's strengths.

The following diagram gives an example of how self-evaluation and coping skills combined with brainstorming and research can result in achievable career goals and dreams for an AD/HD or LD teen.

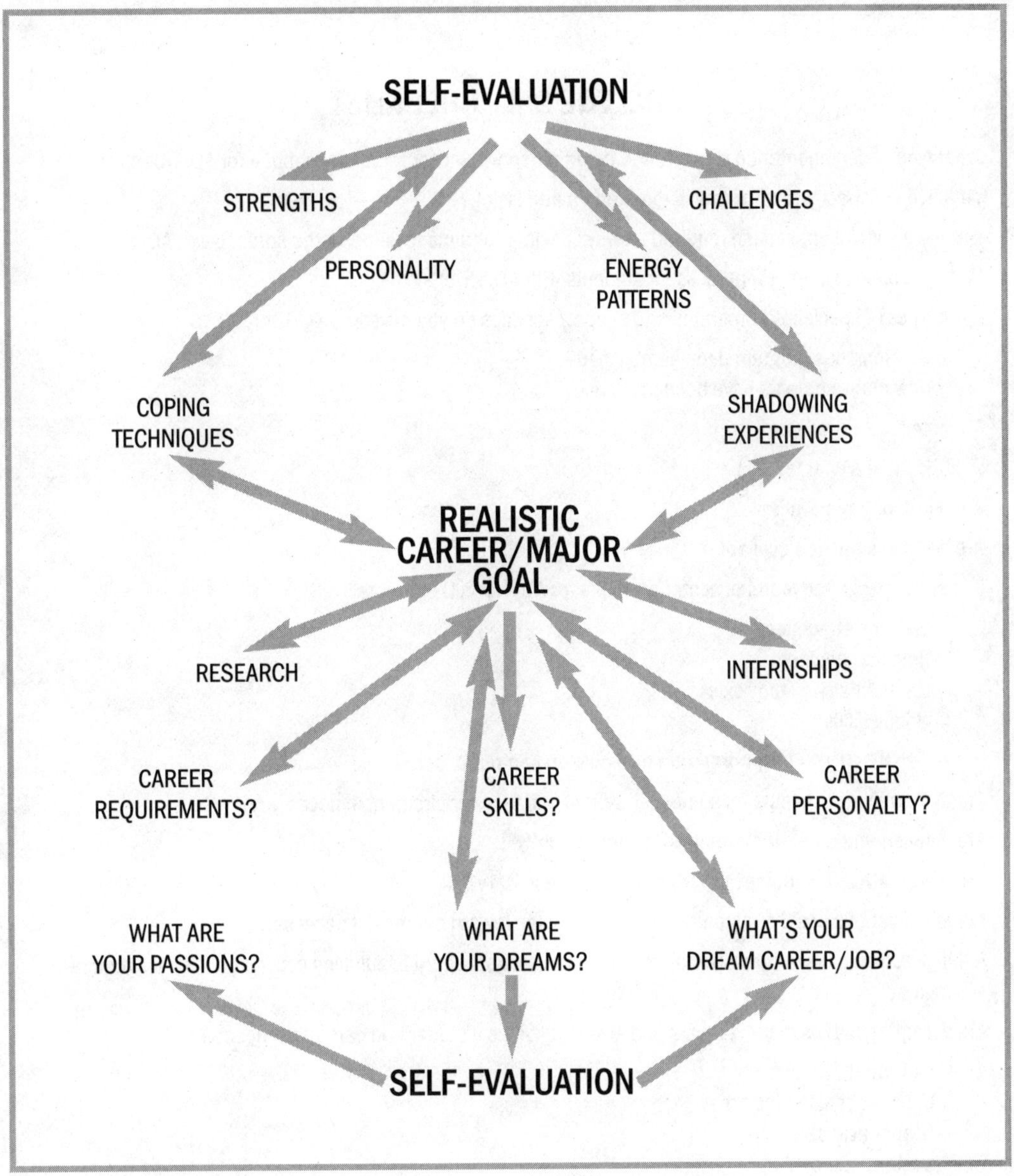
SELF-EVALUATION
STRENGTHS
CHALLENGES
PERSONALITY
ENERGY PATTERNS
COPING TECHNIQUES
SHADOWING EXPERIENCES
REALISTIC CAREER/MAJOR GOAL
RESEARCH
INTERNSHIPS
CAREER REQUIREMENTS?
CAREER SKILLS?
CAREER PERSONALITY?
WHAT ARE YOUR PASSIONS?
WHAT ARE YOUR DREAMS?
WHAT'S YOUR DREAM CAREER/JOB?
SELF-EVALUATION

COLLEGE CALL CHECKLIST

What type of documentation is needed to be admitted with accommodations made for AD/HDorLD?

What type of speciqalized testing is required for admission?

Is there a special application required for any special programs to Isupport the student with AD/HDorLD?

Is there a special interview process for students with AD/HDorLD?

What types of specialized programs and support services do you have for AD/HDorLD?

- How long has program been established?
- How many students have been in service?

Are note takers available?

- Is there a charge?

Are books on tape available?

Are textbooks on tape available?

Is there a specialized learning center available for AD/HDorLD students?

- Learning strategies
- Time management
- Test taking and study skills
- Writing skills

Is there an AD/HD&LD support group available on campus?

Are there waivers available for some high school entrance requirement, if necessary?

Are untimed entrance exams allowed for admission?

Are there waivers for courses toward degrees, if necessary?

Are modifications or substitutions allowed for courses toward degrees, if necessary?

Are high school college-prep special education courses accepted as fulfilling college admissions requirements?

Are accommodations made for tests and exams taken as a student on campus, if needed?

- Individually proctored?
- Untimed or extended time?
- Reader available?
- Scribe available?
- Computers available?

Is one-on-one tutoring available?

- How easy it is to obtain a tutor?
- Is there a cost?
- What is the typical cost?

(Continued)

Is counseling available?

Is academic mentoring available?

When visiting campus:

- Ask if it is possible to meet with a present student with AD/HD or LD characteristics similar to yours?
- Attend some classes.
- Meet with the support staff.
- Spend the night in the dorm and verify if you can deal with the noise and still study well.

The gifted and talented

It is estimated that 5% of the United States student population is considered gifted. The exceptionally gifted student (who may be years younger than other college applicants) requires additional support from the educational community. This support can be in the form of the availability of specialized classes and mentors as early as middle school. These programs provide very specialized accelerated curriculum and counseling that often allow early high school graduation (by several years) and therefore, early admission to college.

For further information, please also consult the honors program section earlier in this book.

COLLEGE CALL CHECKLIST

Within specialized programs for the top scholars is there:

- Specialized counseling?
- Special mentoring with top faculty/administrators?
- Group activities?
- Is there a community service component involved?

What mentoring programs are available?

What are the summer opportunities for top scholars?

How many prior students have you had here with these exceptional gifts and several years younger?

- Did they stay at this college through graduation?
- Is there specialized counseling available?
- If the student stays in the dorm,
  - Is a single room available?
  - Or specially selected and counseled room mate?
- Specialized mentoring available?
- Research opportunities and funding available for students younger than 18?
- How is transportation handled for students under 16?
- How will the college handle the specialized safety issues of a student who is chronologically much younger than academic peers?

Due to the student being under 18 years old, how does the college deal with the confidentiality regulations and parents?

Chapter 9

Those Last Few Minutes

- ✔ To go techie or not
- ✔ Budgeting 101
- ✔ Packing for college
- ✔ First aid for parents

For many of you, leaving for college will be the first time that you will be on your own. You'll have to figure out what you want to bring with you and what you need to buy. Also, this will probably be the first time in your life that you'll have to watch how much you spend. Therefore, this last chapter will focus on the odds and ends that you need to straighten out the summer before you leave for college.

Also, let's not forget that this is a brand-new experience for parents as well. Seeing your child getting ready to go away to college is a very emotional moment. As parents, we are proud to see our children go to college. We dream of our children becoming adults and establishing themselves in very promising careers. However, for many parents, this is the first time that they'll be on their own. The empty nest syndrome can be quite a shock, and parents will have alot to get used to as well.

To go techie or not

About 80% of students do have their own computers on campus. There is no hard and fast rule. Student computer labs are open from 8 a.m. to 11 p.m. but:

- *That's not when most students do their work. Two a.m. is usually peak creative time.*
- *Those labs get crowded at deadline time, quarter break and exam week. You'll never see so many interested, scholarly students in one room.*
- *Your friends become your enemies. That's what it feels like when you have a huge paper on Thermodynamics due the next morning and your friend won't let you use his laptop.*

Professors expect you to be computer literate and proficient. Assignments for research on the Internet are the norm. Some colleges even have lecture halls wired for laptop ports.

Budgeting 101

Contact the Bursar's Office to find out about different payment plans and any tuition cost control options that might be available.

Check with your insurance agent to see if your homeowner's policy covers the contents of your teen's dorm room. See if you need a special rider for his/her computer or musical instrument.

If your student moves to a Greek House or off-campus apartment, you or your teen might need separate renter's insurance. Check with your insurance agent to verify your coverage. Your teen's possessions and clothing need to be insured. The unexpected does happen.

There will be summer orientation weekends and other days for you and your teen to attend. First year summer orientation sessions are very helpful both for the student and parents. This is the specialized time set aside for freshmen and their families to ask detailed questions about living at a particular university. Attend. It's worth the time and effort, and you will have fun.

Make an address and date book for your child with family addresses, phone numbers, e-mail addresses and birthdays. A new household is starting.

This will be the first time that many teens will be living on their own. It is important that they act wisely with regard it to what they spend money on.

Teach your teen how to balance a checkbook, how to create a budget, and how to act in a financially responsible manner.

Some independent scholarships do not announce awards until August or September. Follow up on those, if necessary.

It might be a good idea for parents to send money monthly to their teen instead of just once or twice a semester. Also consider opening up a checking or college credit union account at college. Discuss handling finances, and the expectations and limitations of budgets—both yours and the student's.

Tell your teen to be aware of credit card companies who prey on college students. Unsolicited phone calls by credit card companies to dorms are the rule rather than the exception. Explain the pitfalls of credit cards including a damaged credit rating that will prevent them qualifying for a car loan or renting an apartment

In addition, watch out for scams aimed at incoming freshmen such as offers for ID cards not originating from the college. University ID cards are usually handled at freshmen orientation or at the beginning of the year when you check into your dorm.

Be prepared for the cost of the July/August spending the first year. You're starting a new household and this willl be costly.

> "The best high school graduation gifts mean nothing at the time: a daily calendar, a prepaid calling card, a dry erase board, an instruction booklet on how to do laundry, and a small packet of tissues."
>
> Kim, student

Students involved in special activities such as early fall sports or band will often be required to start school earlier than other freshmen. Many schools have freshmen come several days early for special freshman-only programs.

You will receive information from the residential life office either at freshman orientation or in the mail. You will then be able to make decisions on refrigerator rental or purchase, what size sheets you will have to buy and what elese is needed to live in a dorm.

Your food, cooking, microwave, and refrigerator needs will depend, in part, on the meal plan choices at your university. Some will offer the freshmen fail-safe plan of 21 meals a week (3 meals per day) or up to five meals a day. There is also the plan of only seven evening meals per week. This will mean cooking or finding food for yourself.

Often, college is the first time your child will get sick away from home. Usually it's just the normal illnesses. Discuss which medications work for normal first- aid and medical self-care and send him/her off to school with the basics for fevers, aches, pains, and cuts.

Here is a sample packing list of things that should get you thinking of items you'll need to bring with you:

ITEM

ITEM

TOILERIES		"DORM-WARE"		SCHOOL SUPPLIES	
Scissors		sheets		bulletin board	
dental floss		pillows		pencils, pens, erasers, etc.	
toothpaste		towels		staples	
toothbrush		blanket		tape	
soap/soap dish		Alarm clock		ruler	
sunscreen		surge protectors, 1–3		pencil sharpener	
deodorant		extension cord, several		3-hole punch	
razor/blades/electric		light bulbs		paper clips	
shaving cream		flashlight		rubber bands	
shampoo		batteries		notebooks	
hair dryer		storage boxes		envelopes	
vitamins		ironing board		stamps	
aspirin		hangers		address book	
Band-Aids—flexible		CD rack		calendar—wall	
thermometer		tools, (hammer, screwdriver)		planner/personal	
Eyeglasses/cases/contacts		telephone		calculator	
sewin gkit		Answering machine		dictionary	
		iron—travel		Thesaurus	
		laundry basket/bag			
		detergent			

IDENTIFICATION

Driver's License		
Social Security Card		
Passport		
Checkbook		

(Continued)

ITEM

ITEM		NEED
THINGS TO DO BEFORE LEAVING		
Physical for University		
Medical Insurance card		
Eye Doctor		
Dentist		

A word on safety

A good dose of common sense in all situations goes a long way. You already know that you should never walk at night alone. If you are at the library and it's late, call campus security to get you back to your dorm. Here are some other things, that you already know:

Look around you before you enter your dorm .

Register your bike. Get whatever type of bike lock your campus police recommends, and use it.

Keep your dorm room locked. Most reported thefts occur when students do not lock their dorm room doors.

Know where the emergency phones are located on any path you normally travel.

Try not to be too predictable in the times and routes you take during your daily and weekly schedules.

Don't put your drink down at a party or at a bar. If you have any questions about what is in your drink, get rid of it.

Let people know where you are going and whom you will be with.

Call campus security or the police any time you are unsure about your safety.

Binge drinking is defined as five drinks or beers in an hour for a male and four drinks or beers in an hour for a female. Binge drinking kills. During 1997, more than 40 college students died in alcohol related incidents. In addition, alcohol is involved in 90% of the violent incidents on campuses.

"We're not putting all the blame on students," says Sandra Hoover, Ph.D., Deputy Director of the Robert Woods Johnson Foundation's Matter of Degree Program. "Everyone has a roll in reducing high-risk drinking: sellers of alchol, parents, and alumni. Unfortunately, there's an attitude that binge drinking is a rite of pasage and relatively harmless, and that it goes with college life."

The last few seconds

On moving day, make sure all medications are available and any special needs have been taken care of. Bring an assortment of tools for those unpredictable tasks that happen when you move anywhere.

Welcome to college. Most likely, your room will be unfit for most living creatures. Remember that the last person who lived in your room was in a hurry to go home last spring. So on moving day, allow time to clean up before unpacking.

PARENTS CORNER

Leave a broom, dust pan, dust mop and some cleaning supplies for your student to use.

As your teen packs up everything to take to school, let him/her know how very proud you are of him/her. Besides being the truth, it helps with the inevitable homesickness that comes sooner or later.

First aid for parents

This section gives you an idea of what life will be like once your child heads off to college. Each experience is different, but the pattern is the same. Enjoy the journey—it's far from over.

Just when you thought all the paperwork was done, more arrives.Now you'll have keep track of housing receipts, refrigerator rental, and so on. You will also start receiving mail from your child's university and from its parents' organization.

Scrutinize the Bursar's bill closely. Even colleges can make mistakes.

Don't throw away the applications and information for the other schools that accepted your son/daughter. In case he/she decides to transfer, they may come in handy.

Make arrangements early for a place to stay if you are planning to attend Parent's Weekend. Lodging fills up quickly when nearby colleges have events. If you get the date, book in the summer.

A gift idea for your student is a subscription to a professional journal in his/her area of interest.

Be prepared in your child's first year to mentally "hit a wall" anywhere from four to six weeks into the first semester. That first semester is always difficult, and sometimes your child may feel overwhelmed and have major doubts if he/she will survive until quarter break, much less the whole semester. This is normal and nothing to worry about. This is also a good time for lots of care packages from home.

Also be prepared for his/her grades to slip a bit. This is to be expected no matter how well your child prepares for college. Professor's comments might seem very critical compared to how their high school teachers treated him/her. Even though it's normal, it's not easy to adjust to. It can be a very traumatic experience. Send those care packages.

If you don't have the time to make care packages yourself, some companies, residence life, or campus service organizations provide care packages for a fee.

Keep your child in mind when you are decorating for the holidays. A dorm room is nothing like your own home and some decorations will make a lonely room a much homier place.

Send stamps and rolls of quarters.

You may not hear from your child as much as you think you would or like, but this is normal. They are experiencing being on their own for the first time and you need to be there for them when needed, not hassling them to call.

Every year, financial aid has to be reapplied for. You must fill out the FAFSA three more times. Check with your child's school for the deadline. Some scholarships must be reapplied for, or at the very least, a renewal form signed. Federal loans and grants are the same. Help your child keep track of these very important things.

Remember all those things that you loaded up in August? By spring, it's almost time to bring it home. Some schools provide summer storage for items too big to transport.

Highlights

- ★ Computers and the Internet are the wave of the future. A college's access to the Internet and the quality of its computer labs are major factors that determine how good a college is. Look into this very closely.
- ★ You'll also have to start managing your own money. You can do with it what you want but whose is going to replace it if it runs out? You will have to keep a watchful eye not only on spending money, but book money, scholarship information, and student loans. Ask your parents to show you simple budgeting so you're not broke by October.
- ★ Make sure to use the checklist provided of items to bring with you to college. This isn't like going on vacation or camp. You are moving out on your own and won't have Mom or Dad to help you if you forget to bring something.

★ Parents, this is a new journey for you as well. You will be excited and terrified for your child as well as for yourself. Keep in mind that once the initial shock is over, it will be a wonderful time for all of you.

Appendix

College Call Checklist

COLLEGE NAME ______________________________

Contact person: ______________________________

Phone number: ______________________________

Fax number: ______________________________

Internet address: ______________________________

Admissions address: ______________________________

____

____

ENTRANCE REQUIREMENTS

High School courses required? ______________________________

____

____

____

Which college admissions tests are required? ____________________

____

____

____

Deadlines for test scores? ____________________

____

ACADEMIC AREA/MAJORS

What are the university's specialties? ____________________

____

____

How many students are in these specialties? ____________________

____

FRESHMAN CLASS

What is a typical freshman schedule like? ____________________

____

What is the retention rate for freshmen? ____________________

What are average SAT/ACT scores for in-coming freshmen? __________

____

What percent of graduates go on to Graduate School? ____________

Do graduate students teach freshmen? ____________

What is the percentage of class that graduates in 4 years? ____________

What is the percentage of class that takes 5+ years to complete undergraduate work? ____________

APPLICATION INFO

Application method: ____________

Traditional paper application? ____________

Included in View Book? ____________

Internet online application? ____________

On-Disk application? Any extra fees involved? ____________

____

Which application method does the university prefer? ____________

____

Does the university allow use of The Common Application? ____________

Essay required with application? ____________

How many? ____________

Deadline(s) for application ____________

____

Application fee, how much? ______________________

____

University-specific Financial Aid Estimator included? ________

LIBRARY

What are the library's hours? ______________________

Computerized book catalog? ______________________

Networked to any outside library resources? __________

____

RANKINGS

U.S. News & World Report ______________________

The Gourman Report ______________________

Money Magazine ______________________

INTERDISCIPLINARY STUDIES

Available? ______________________

Are the programs within specific curriculum areas, such as in sciences? _____

____

(or) Across all programs ______________________________

(or) University defined______________________________

Degree available ______________________________

OPTIONS FOR UNDECIDED MAJORS

Special academic counseling? ______________________________

Special mentoring available? ______________________________

EXTRACURRICULAR ACTIVITIES

What are the athletic and recreational facilities available? __________

____

____

Sports: intramural, club ______________________________

____

____

Sports, varsity (Consult student's high school coach(s) for specific information/methods of seeking athletic scholarships: e.g., references, play videos, etc.)

____

____

____

Orchestra/Band for music/nonmusic majors ______________________

____

Theater for theater/nontheater majors ______________________

____

COMPUTER INFORMATION

IBM or MAC based? ______________________

Campus networked? ______________________

Dorm rooms networked? ______________________

Through phone lines or direct network cabling in room? ____________

Internet connection capabilities? ______________________

Computer labs? ______________________

Location and how many? ______________________

____

What are hours of operation? ______________________

CAMPUS INFO

Population______________________

If there is a rural area, how far is it to the nearest city and how do students get there? ______________________

Where is the closest major airport to campus? ______________________

What is the percentage of Greek life (Fraternities and Sororoties) on campus?

What method of transportation do students use to get around campus? ____

What are the regulations for freshmen regarding cars? ______________

Does the university have its own bus system and what are its hours of operaion? ______________________________

Health services available? ______________________________

HOUSING IN GENERAL

Voice Mail available? ______________________________

Single-sex dorms available? ______________________________

Coed dorms, how structured? ______________________________

Freshman segregated? ____________________

What is supplied in dorm rooms? Can you use lofts? ____________________

____

____

____

Where are Laundromats? ____________________

How are roommates assigned? ____________________

____

Refrigerator rental? ____________________

Are there smoke free rooms/dorms available? ____________________

Is air conditioning available for students who have certified medical needs, i.e., severe allergies, asthma, etc.? ____________________

MEAL PLANS

How many meals available per day and on which days? (Some universities only offer evening meal) ____________________

____

What are the other food options available on campus? ____________________

____

PROSPECTIVE STUDENT VISITS

Days and hours ____________________

Special weekends? ____________________

Arranged? ____________________

Special places to stay near or on campus? ____________________

____

Campus map? ____________________

Map of area? ____________________

TUITION AND FINANCIAL AID

Tuition ____________________

Room and Board ____________________

Fees, miscellaneous and books ____________________

____

Any tuition-ceiling guarantee programs available? ____________________

Which forms are needed for financial aid? ____________________

____

Deadline(s) ____________________

When are deposits due for freshmen (a.k.a. First Years)? ____________________

____

How much? ______________________________________

What types of payment plans are available? ______________________

____

If this is a state-supported university: How much are the out-of-state fees? __

____

Does that state have a reciprocity agreement with yours, whereby those out-of-state fees may be waived? ______________________________

Are there any circumstances in which the out-of-state fees may be waived? __

____

____

Glossary

ACT (American College Testing) is a college admission test based on the curriculum areas of English, Math, Social Studies, Reading Skills and Scientific Reasoning.

AP (Advanced Placement Program) specialized national course work administered by the College Board that allows students to take college level courses while in high school. If the student scores high enough on the national exam, college credit may be granted for the course.

CLEP (College Level Exam Program) allows testing for possible college credit for beginning college courses.

Common Application a college application available for use for a number of colleges. If the student applies to colleges that use the Common Application, then theoretically only this one application needs to be used. Most colleges do not make use of the common application.

Correspondence Courses course work available through universities. Students work on these courses independently with the only interaction between the student and professor is through the mail or computer.

Dual/shared enrollment Students are enrolled and attend high school and college at the same time.

Expected Family Cost (EFC) is the amount of the cost of attending college that the family is expected to pay. EFC is computed by a national formula determined by filing the Free Application for Federal Student Aid (FAFSA).

Extracurricular activities activities outside of normal classroom courses—such as clubs, volunteering, drama, art and/or sports.

FAFSA (Free Application for Federal Student Financial Aid) which determines the family's expected contribution toward the cost of going to college.

Financial Aid funds made available to students to pay for college from sources outside the family. Examples are loans, grants or scholarships.

Financial Planning for College long and short term planning for families to accommodate the expenses associated with college attendance.

Honors Programs University programs allow qualified students to work at high academic levels. Most programs have specialized courses, small-sized classes and opportunities for research. Some have special housing features.

Independent Study whereby students works outside class (with the guidance of a teacher or mentor) to cover course work.

IB (International Baccalaureate Program) available in high schools who have applied and qualified to offer this specialized curriculum. The program is available in the United States and internationally. IB allows college level subject area curriculum based on global interpretation to be taught in high school.

Joint cooperative course program partnership between high school and local colleges whereby the college grants credit for certain courses taught at the high school.

NAIA (National Association of Intercollegiate Athletes) Association that governs interaction between college coaches and student players at small schools.

NCAA (National Collegiate Athletic Association) Association that governs interaction between college coaches and student players at large schools.

NSCAA (National Small College Athletic Association) Association that governs interaction between college coaches and student players at very small schools.

PLAN Preliminary form of SAT, taken in the Freshman or Sophomore year.

PSAT (Preliminary Scholastic Assessment Test) preparatory test for the SAT. Offered once a year in October. Sophomores may take this test for practice. For Juniors taking this test and scoring high enough, the PSAT serves as the possible admission to the National Merit Scholarship Program.

Performing Arts vocal music, instrumental music, drama, musical theater and dance.

Profile specialized financial aid form required by some schools available through the College Scholarship Services (CSS) a subsidiary of the College Board.

Resume A 4-year list of work, extracurricular and award experiences that will be used for most college and scholarship applications.

Room and Board cost of dorm room and meal plan.

SAT I (Scholarship Assessment Test) one of two main college admissions tests.

SAT II Achievement Tests subject area achievement tests required by some colleges.

Solid Top 5 Top Core Courses - English/Language Arts, Math, Science, Social Studies/History, and Foreign Language.

Student Aid Report (SAR) report that is generated after filing FAFSA that gives the Expected Family Contribution (EFC).

TOEFL (Test of English as a Foreign Language) testing required in addition to SAT or ACT, if English is not the native language.

Tuition cost of attending college classes.

TWE (Test of Written English) College Board test required by some colleges.

Visual Arts painting, drawing, sculpting, computer animation, architecture are examples.

Web sites, college vast majority of colleges have web sites - where you can start your research and confirm details.

References

Adderholt-Elliott; Miriam. *Perfectionism: What's Bad About Being Too Good? (Revised and Updated Edition)* Minneapolis: Free Spirit Publishing, 1999.

Adler, JoeAnne. *Women's Colleges*. New York: Prentice Hall, 1994.

Allen, Joseph. *10 Minute Guide To Choosing A College*. New York: Macmillan, 1996.

Alvino, James; and Editors of Gifted Children Monthly. *Parents' Guide to Raising a Gifted Child: Recognizing and Developing Your Child's Potential*. New York: Ballentine Books, 1985.

Anderson, Shaun. *Countdown to College*. Mesa: Bluebird Publishing, 1997.

Andrews, Linda Landis. *How To Choose A College Major*. Chicago: VGM Career Horizons, 1998.

Antonoff, Steven. *The College Finder*. New York: Ballantine Books, 1993.

Antonoff, Steven and Friedemann, Marie A. *College Match: A Blue Print for Choosing the Best School for You! 5th Edition*. Alexandria: Octaneron Associates, 1997.

ARCO. *High School Entrance Exams*. New York: Macmillan Press, annual editions.

ARCO. *The RightCollege*. New York: Prentice Hall, annual editions.

Basco, Monica. *Never Good Enough: Freeing Yourself From The Chains of Perfectionism*. The Free Press, 1998.

Bauld, Harry. *On Writing the College Application Essay*. New York: Barnes and Noble Books, 1978.

Benson, Peter L.; Galbraith, Judy; Espeland, Pamela. *What Kids Need to Succeed: Proven, Practical Ways to Raise Good Kids (Revised, Expanded, and Updated Edition)*. Minneapolis: Free Spirit Publishing, 1998.

Benson, Peter L.; Galbraith, Judy; Espeland, Pamela. *What Teens Need to Succeed: Proven, Practical Ways to Sahpe Your Own Future*. Minneapolis: Free Spirit Publishing.

Boyer, Ernest C.; Boyer, Paul. *College: The Undergrad Experience in America*. New York: Harper and Row Publishers, 1987.

Boyer, Ernest L. *Smart Parents Guide to College: The 10 most important factors for students and parents when choosing a college*. Princeton, NJ: Peterson's, 1996.

Bromwell, Perry; Gensler, Howard. *The Student Athlete's Handbook: The Complete Guide to Success*. New York: John Wiley & Sons, Inc., 1997.

Cahn, Victor L. *A Thinking Student's Guide to College*. Norwell: Christopher Publishing House, 1988.

Cassidy, Daniel J. *The Scholarship Book*. Englewood Cliffs: Prentice Hall, 1996.

Cobain, Bev. *When Nothing Matters Anymore: A Survival Guide for Depressed Teens*. Minneapolis: Free Spirit Publishing.

Coburn, Karen Levin and Treeger, Madge Lawrence. *Letting Go: A Parents' Guide to Understanding The College Years*. (Third Edition) New York: HarperPerennial, 1997.

Cochrane, Kelly. *Researching Colleges On The World Wide Web*. New York: Franklin Watts, 1997.

Cole, Wendy; Mitchell, Emily; Rutherford, Megan. "How to Make A Better Student," TIME. October 19, 1998.

College Entrance Examination Board. *The College Handbook for Transfer Students, 1997 Seventh Edition*. New York: College Entrance Examination Board, 1997.

Cummings, Rhoda; Fisher, Gary. *The Survival Guide for Teenagers with LD (Learning Differences)*. Minneapolis: Free Spirit Publishing.

Dahlstrom, Lorraine M. *Writing Down The Days: 365 Creative Journaling Ideas for Young People*. Minneapolis: Free Spirit Publishing.

Davis, Kristen. *Financing College*. Washington, D.C.: Keplinger Books, 1996.

Delisle, James R., *Gifted Kids Speak Out: Hundreds of Kids Ages 6-13 Talk About School, Friends, Their Families, and The Future*. Minneapolis: Free Spirit Publishing.

Drum, Alice. *Funding A College Education*. Boston: Howard Business School Press, 1996.

Dublan, Rachel; Sippy, Shana. *The College Woman's Handbook*. New York: Workman Publishing, 1995.

Duvall, Lynn. *Respecting Our Differences: A Guide to Getting Along in a Changing World*. Minneapolis: Free Spirit Publishing.

Edwards, Stephanie. *101 Things A College Girl Should Know, From A Big Sister Who's Been There*. Kansas City: Andrews and McMeel, 1996.

Ehrenhaft, George. *Writing A Successful College Application Essay*. New York: Barrron's, 1993.

Ehrlich, Virginia Z. *Gifted Children: A Guide for Parents & Teachers*. Englewood Cliff, NJ: Prentice-Hall, Inc., 1982.

Erickson, Judith B. *1998-1999 Directory of American Youth Organizations: A Guide to 500 Clubs, Groups, Troops, Teams, Societies, Lodges, and More for Young People (Updated and Revised Seventh Edition)*. Minneapolis: Free Spirit Publishing, 1998.

Erlbach, Arlene. *Worth The Risk: True Stories About Risk Takers Plus How You Can Be One, Too*. Minneapolis: Free Spirit Publishing.

Espeland, Pamela; Verdick, Elizabeth. *Making Every Day Count: Daily Readings for Young People on Solving Problems, Setting Goals, & Feeling Good About Yourself*. Minneapolis: Free Spirit Publishing.

Espeland, Pamela; Wallner, Rosemary. *Making The Most of Today: Daily Readings for Young People on Self-Awareness, Ceativity & Self-Esteem*. Minneapolis: Free Spirit Publishing.

Estell, Doug; Satchwell, Michele L.; Wright, Patricia S. *Reading Lists For College-Bound Students: Get A Head Start on College Success! 2nd edition*. New York: Macmillan, 1993.

Everett, Carole J. *ARCO The Performing Arts Major's College Guide: Dance, Drama, Music, 3rd Edition*. New York, Macmillan Reference USA, 1998.

Farr, J. Michael. *America's Top Jobs for People Without a Four-Year Degree*. Indianapolis, IN: JIST Works.

Farr, J. Michael. *America's Top Medical, Education, and Human Services Jobs*. Indianapolis, IN: JIST Works.

Featherstone, Bonnie D. and Reilly, Jill M. *College Comes Sooner Than You Think! The Essential College Planning Guide for High School Students and Their Families*. Dayton, OH: Ohio Psychology Press, 1990.

Finch, Peter; Marshall, Delia. *How to Raise Kids without Going Broke: The Complete Financial Guide for Parents*. Avon Books, 1999.

Fisher, Gary; Cummings, Rhonda. *When Your Child Has LD (Learning Differences): A Survival Guide for Parents*. Minneapolis: Free Spirit Publishing.

Fiske, Edward B. *The Fiske Guide To College*. New York: Random House, 1998.

Fiske, Edward. B. *How To Get Into the Right College*. New York: Times Books, 1998.

Flick, Grad L. *ADD/ADHD Behavior-Change Resource Kit: Ready-to-Use Strategies & Activities for Helping Children with Attention Deficit Disorder*. Minneapolis: Free Spirit Publishing.

Fogg, Neeta, P.; Harrington, Paul E.; Harrington, Thomas. *The College Majors Handbook: The Actual Jobs, Earnings, and Trends for Graduates of 60 College Majors*. Indianapolis, IN: JIST Works, 1999.

Folkers, Gladys; Englemann, Jeanne. *Taking Charge of My Mind & Body: A Girl's Guide to Outsmarting Alcohol, Drug, Smoking, and Eating Problems*. Minneapolis: Free Spirit Publishing.

Galbraith, Judy and Delisle, Jim. *The Gifted Kid's Survival Guide: A Teen Handbook*. Minneapolis: Free Spirit Publishing Inc., 1996.

Gelband, Scott; Kubale, Catherine; and Schom, Eric. *Your College Application*. New York: College Entrance Examination Board, 1984.

Giddan, Norman and Vallongo, Sally. *Parenting Through The College Years: From Application to Graduation*. Charlotte, VT: Williamson Publishing, 1988.

Gootman, Marilyn E. *When A Friend Dies: A Book for Teens About Grieving and Healing*. Minneapolis: Free Spirit Publishing.

Gorder, Cheryl. Home Education Resource Guide, 4th Edition. Mesa, AZ: Blue Bird Publishing, 1996.

Gourman, Jack. *The Gourman Report: A Rating of Undergraduate Programs in American and International Universities*. Los Angeles, CA: National Education Standards, annual.

Grant, Janet E. *The Young Person's Guide To Becoming A Writer*. Minneapolis: Free Spirit Publishing.

Greene, Howard and Mintar, Robert. *Scaling the Ivy Wall in the 90's*. Boston: Little, Brown, and Company, 1994.

Guernsey, Lisa. *College Education*. Alexandria: Octaneron Associates, 1997.

Guernsey, Lisa. College.Edu: *On-Line Resources for the Cyber-Savvy Student*. Alexandria, VA: Octamoron Associates, Inc., 1997.

Hartman, Kenneth E. *Internet Guide for College Bound Students*. New York: College Entrance Examination Board, 1996.

Heacox, Diane. *Up From Underachievement: How Teachers, Students and Parents Can Work Together to Promote Student Success*. Minneapolis: Free Spirit Publishing.

Hendricks, Gay. *Conscious Breathing: Breathwork for Health, Stress Relief and Personal Mastery*. New York: Bantum Books, 1995.

Hernandez, Michele A. *A is for Admissions*. New York: Warner Books, 1997.

Hipp, Earl. *Fighting Invisible Tigers: A Stress Management Guide for Teens*. Minneapolis: Free Spirit Publishing.

Huegel, Kelly. *Young People and Chronic Illness: True Stories, Help and Hope*. Minneapolis: Free Spirit Publishing.

Isdell, Wendy. *The Chemy Called Al*. Minneapolis: Free Spirit Publishing.

Isdell, Wendy. *A Gebra Named Al*. Minneapolis: Free Spirit Publishing.

Jacobs, Thomas A. *What Are My Rights? 95 Questions and Answers About Teens and the Law*. Minneapolis: Free Spirit Publishing.

JIST Works, Inc. *The Enhanced Occupational Outlook Handbook*. Indianapolis, IN: JIST Works, Inc.

JIST Works, Inc. *Young Person's Occupational Outlook Handbook*. Indianapolis, IN: JIST Works, Inc., 1998.

Kaplan Scholarships. New York: Simon and Schuster, 1997.

Karnes, Frances A.; Bean, Suzanne M. *Girls and Young Women Leading the Way: 20 True Stories About Leadership*. Minneapolis: Free Spirit Publishing.

Karnes, Frances A.; Bean, Suzanne M. *Girls and Young Women Entrepreneurs: True Stories About Starting and Running a Business Plus How You Can Do It Yourself*. Minneapolis: Free Spirit Publishing.

Karnes, Frances A.; Bean, Suzanne M. *Girls and Young Women Inventing: Twenty True Stories About Inventors Plus How You Can Be One Yourself*. Minneapolis: Free Spirit Publishing.

Kaufman, Gershen. *Stick Up For Yourself! Every Kid's Guide to Personal Power and Positive Self-Esteem (Revised and Updated Edition)*. Minneapolis: Free Spirit Publishing, 1999.

Kaye, Evelyn and Gardner, Janet. *College Bound*. New York: College Entrance Examination Board, 1989.

Kerr, Barbara A. *Smart Girls—Gifted Women*. Dayton, OH: Ohio Psychology Press, 1985.

Kesslar, Oreon. *Financial Aids for Higher Education*. Dubuque: Wm. C. Brown Publishers, 1986.

Kranz, Linda. *Through My Eyes: A Journal for Teens*. Minneapolis: Free Spirit Publishing.

Kravets, Marybeth; Wax, Imy F. *The Princeton Review: K&W Guide to Colleges For the Learning Disabled*. New York, Random House, Inc., 1997.

Lauren, Jill. *Succeeding With LD: 20 True Stories About Real People with LD (Learning Differences)*. Minneapolis: Free Spirit Publishing.

Leider, Anna. *Don't Miss Out: The Ambitious Student's Guide to Financial Aid*. Alexandria, VA: Octameron Associates, annual.

Leonhardt, Mary. *99 Ways to Get Kids to Love Reading*. Minneapolis: Free Spirit Publishing.

Leonhardt, Mary. *99 Ways to Get Kids to Love Writing*. Minneapolis: Free Spirit Publishing.

Levey, Marc; Blanco, Michael; Jones, W. Terrell. *How to Succeed on a Majority Campus: A Guide for Minority Students*. New York: Wadsworth Publishing Company, 1998.

Lewis, Barbara A. *Kids With Courage: True Stories About Young People Making a Difference*. Minneapolis: Free Spirit Publishing.

Lewis, Barbara A. *The Kid's Guide to Service Projects: Over 500 Service Ideas for Young People Who Want to Make a Difference*. Minneapolis: Free Spirit Publishing.

Lewis, Barbara A. *The Kid's Guide to Social Action: How to Solve the Social Problems You Choose-and Turn Creative Thinking into Positive Action (Revised, Expanded, Updated Edition)*. Minneapolis: Free Spirit Publishing.

Lewis, Barbara A. *What Do You Stand For? A Kid's Guide to Building Character*. Minneapolis: Free Spirit Publishing.

Ludden, LaVerne. *Ludden's Adult Guide to Colleges and Universities*. Indianapolis, IN: JIST Works, Inc.

Margolin, Judith B. *Financing A College Education*. New York: Plenum Press, 1989.

Marshall, Brian; Ford, Wendy. *The Secrets of Getting Better Grades: Study Smarter, Not Harder*. Indianapolis: IN: JIST Works, Inc.

Mayher, Bill. *The College Admission Mystique*. New York: Noonday Press, 1998.

Maze, Marilyn; Mayall, Donald; Farr, J. Michael. *The Enhanced Guide for Occupational Exploration*. Indianapolis, IN: JIST Works, Inc.

McCoy, Kathleen. *Understanding Your Teenager's Depression: Issues, Insights & Practical Guidance for Parents*. Minneapolis: Free Spirit Publishing, 1998.

McCutcheon, Randall. *Get Off My Brain: A Survival Guide for Lazy Students (Revised and Updated Editon)*. Minneapolis: Free Spirit Publishing.

McGinty, Sarah Myers. *The College Application Essay*. New York: The College Board, 1997.

McMurchie, Susan. *Understanding LD (Learning Differences): A Curriculum to Promote LD Awareness, Self-Esteem, and Coping Skills in Students Ages 8–13*. Minneapolis: Free Spirit Publishing.

Mirriam-Goldberg, Caryn. *Write Where You Are: How to use Writing to Make Sense of Your Life*. Minneapolis: Free Spirit Publishing, 1999.

Money Guide, "Best College Buys Now," annual.

National Occupational Information Coordinating Committee of JIST Works, Inc. *Creating Your High School Portfolio: An Interactive Career School and Life Planning Workbook*. Indianapolis, IN: JIST Works, Inc., 1998.

Nelson, Richard E.; Galas, Judith C. *The Power To Prevent Suicide: A Guide for Teens Helping Teens*. Minneapolis: Free Spirit Publishing.

Newman, Susan with King, Janet Spencer. *Getting Your Child Into College: What Parents Must Know*. New York: St. Martin's Griffin, 1996.

Nierwenheis, Marjorie. *The Parent's Guide To College Admission*. New York: Kaplan Books, 1992.

Nourse, Kenneth A. *How To Write Your College Application Essay*. Chicago: NTC Business Books, 1994.

Ordovensky, Pat. *College Planning for Dummies*. Chicago: IDG Books Worldwide, 1998.

Ordovensky, Pat. *Getting Into College*. Princeton: Peterson's, 1995.

Otto, Luther B. *Helping Your Child Choose A Career: A Book for Parents, Teachers, Counselors and (even) Students*. Indianapolis, IN: JIST Works, Inc., 1998.

Packer, Alex J. *Bringing Up Parents: The Teenager's Handbook*. Minneapolis: Free Spirit Publishing.

Packer, Alex J. *How Rude! The Teenagers' Guide to Good Manners, Proper Behavior, and Not Grossing People Out*. Minneapolis: Free Spirit Publishing.

Page, Christina. *The Smart Girl's Guide to College*. New York: Noonday Press, 1997.

Paul, Bill. *Getting In*. New York: Addison-Wesley Publishing Company, 1995.

Pendleton, Scott. *The Ultimate Guides To Student Contests*. Minneapolis: Free Spirit Publishing.

Peterson's College and University Almanac. Princeton: Peterson's, annual.

Peterson's College Money Handbook. Princeton: Peterson's, annual.

Peterson's Competitive Colleges: Making the Most of Campus Visits. Princeton: Peterson's, annual.

Peterson's Four Year Colleges. Princeton: Peterson's, annual.

Peterson's Guide to (U.S. Regions). Princeton: Peterson's, annual.

Peterson's Honors Programs. Princeton: Peterson's, annual.

Peterson's Study Abroad. Princeton: Peterson's, annual.

Peterson's Two Year Colleges. Princeton: Peterson's, annual.

Pope, Loren. *The Right College*. New York: Macmillan, 1970.

Quinn, Patricia O.; Stern, Judith M. *Putting on the Brakes: Young People's Guide to Understanding Attention Deficit Hyperactivity Disorder (ADHD)*. Minneapolis: Free Spirit Publishing.

Robinsy, Adam and Katzman, John (Ed.). *Princeton Review: College Admission: Cracking the System*. New York: Villard Books, 1987.

Reilly, Jill M. and Featherstone, Bonnie D. *College Comes Sooner Than You Think!: The College Planning Guide for High School Students and Their Families*. Hawthorne: The Career Press, 1987.

Reischl, Dennis K. *Winning An Athletic Scholarship*. Greendale: WorldSport, 1995.

Robbins, Wendy H. *The Portable College Adviser: A Guide for High School Students*. New York: Franklin Watts, 1995.

Rowe, Fred A. *The Career Connection for College Education: A Guide to College Education and Related Career Opportunities*. Indianapolis, IN: JIST Works, Inc., 1998.

Rowe, Fred A. *The Career Connection for Technical Education: A Guide to Technical and Related Career Opportunities*. Indianapolis, IN: JIST Works, Inc., 1998.

Rubenstone, Sally and Dalby, Sidonia. *College Admissions: A Crash Course for Panicked Parents*. New York: Macmillan, 1998.

Schlachter, Gail Ann and Weber, R. David. *High School Senior's Guide To Merit and Other No-Need Funding*. San Carlos: Reference Service Press, 1996.

Schmitz, Connie C., Galbraith, Judy. *Managing The Social And Emotional Needs of the Gifted: A Teacher's Survival Guide*. Minneapolis: Free Spirit Publishing.

Scott, Robert L. *How to Market Your Student Athlete, Fourth Revised Edition*. Flagler Beach, FL: Athletic Guide Publishing, 1997.

Schumm, Jeanne Shay; Radencih, Marguerite. *School Power: Strategies for Succeeding in School*. Minneapolis: Free Spirit Publishing.

Schwager, Tina; Schuerger, Michele. *Gutsy Girls: Young Women Who Dare*. Minneapolis: Free Spirit Publishing, 1999.

Schwager, Tina; Schuerger, Michele. *The Right Moves: A Girl's Guide to Getting Fit and Feeling Good*. Minneapolis: Free Spirit Publishing.

Schwartz, John. *College Scholarships and Financial Aid*. New Orleans: Wintergreen/Orchard House, Inc., 1995.

Sharpe, Pamela J. *How To Prepare For the TOEFL Test: Test of English as a Foreign Language, Eighth Edition*. New York: Barron's Educational Series, Inc., 1996.

Shields, Charles J. *The College Guide for Parents*. New York: College Entrance Examination Board, 1986.

Spence, Annette. *Campus Bound*. Los Angeles: Price, Stern, Sloan, 1990.

Spohn, David. *Life on the Edge: Parenting a Child with ADD/ADHD*. Minneapolis: Free Spirit Publishing.

Stauss, Susan with Espeland, Pamela. *Sexual Harassment and Teens: A Program for Positive Change*. Minneapolis: Free Spirit Publishing, 1998.

Stein, Deborah. *Curiosity in a Jar*. Minneapolis: Free Spirit Publishing.

Stein, Deborah. *Gratitude For Teens In a Jar: Daily Inspirations...365 Quotes*. Minneapolis: Free Spirit Publishing.

Steinberg, Eve P. *Catholic High School Entrance Examinations*. New York. Macmillan, 1997.

Student Services. *The Minority & Women's Complete Scholarship Book*. Naperville, IL: Sourcebook, Inc., 1998.

Sweetar, Linda and Brown, Carol. *The Art Student's College Guide*. New York: Macmillan, 1996.

Sykes, Charles; Miner, Brad; and Buckley, William (Ed.). *National Review College Guide*. New York: Wolgemuth and Hyatt Publishers, Inc., 1991.

Turner, O'Neal. *The Complete Idiot's Guide to Getting Into College*. Indianapolis: Alpha Books, 1994.

Tyler, Suzette. *Been There Should've Done That! 505 Tips for Making the Most of College*. Haslett, MI: Front Porch Press, 1997.

U.S. News & World Report. "America's Best Colleges," annual.

Walker, Sally Yahnke. *The Survival Guide For Parents of Gifted Kids: How to Understand, Live With, and Stick Up for Your Gifted Child.* Minneapolis: Free Spirit Publishing.

Warren, Christopher. *So You're Going to College.* Chapel Hill: Kilroy Press, 1989.

Webb, James T.; Meekstroth, Elizabeth A; Tolan, Stephanie S. *Guiding the Gifted Child: A Practical Source for Parents and Teachers.* Dayton, OH: Ohio Psychology Press., 1982.

Weldon, Amelie. *Girls Who Rocked The World: Heroines from Sacagawea to Sheryl Swoopes.* Minneapolis: Free Spirit Publishing.

Wilber, Jessica. *Totally Private & Personal: Journaling Ideas for Girls and Young Women.* Minneapolis: Free Spirit Publishing.

World Book Staff. *Stand Up For Your Rights: A Book About Human Rights Written By and For the Young People of the World.* World Books.

Worthington, Janet Farrar and Farrar, Ronald. *The Ultimate College Survival Guide.* Princeton: Peterson's, 1995.

VonGruben, Jill F. "Accepting a Disability," *Parish Family Digest.* July/August 1991.

Index

A
Acceptance, college, 192–193
ACT (American College Testing), 9, 19, 28, 76–77, 122, 146, 167
ADD (Attention Deficit Disorder), 80. *See also* Disabilities, students with
AD/HD (Attention Deficit/Hyperactivity Disorder), 204–207. *See also* Disabilities, students with
Admissions staff, 72, 170–172
Advanced Placement (AP) program, 81–86, 120, 122
American College Testing (ACT), 9, 19, 28, 76–77, 122, 146, 167
AmeriCorps, 112
Applications, college, 175–183
  essays, 172–174
    Internet sites that provide assistance in writing, 174
    steps in writing, 174
  example, 177–178, 180–183
  online, 178–179
  written follow-up to make sure you receive them, 175–176
AP (Advanced Placement) program, 81–86, 120, 122
Athletics
  college admissions based on. *See* Sports and college admissions
  as extracurricular activity, 43–44, 50
Attention Deficit Disorder (ADD), 80. (*continued*)
  See also Disabilities, students with
Attention Deficit/Hyperactivity Disorder (AD/HD), 204–207. *See also* Disabilities, students with
Awards, 43–44

B
Binge drinking, 215
Blindness, 200–201. *See also* Disabilities, students with

C
Campbell Interest and Skill Survey (CISS), 25
Career choices, 24–25
Class ranking, relative unimportance of, 30–33
CLEP (College Level Examination Program), 76–77
College admissions tests, 18–19, 119–122, 167–168. *See also* names of specific tests (such as PSAT, SAT)
  dependence on reading and vocabulary skills, 9
  disabled students, special arrangements for, 80, 198, 200
  use of calculators, 79
College applications. *See* Applications, college
College costs. *See* Costs, college

College Level Examination Program (CLEP), 76–77
College preparation. *See* "grade" entries (Eighth grade; Ninth grade; Tenth grade; Eleventh grade; Twelfth grade); Survival
College selection, 67–75, 123–132
  admissions staff, 72
  checklists, 127–132, 134–135
  comparison list, 73–75
  highly selective schools, 127
  Honors Programs, 132–135
  performing arts, 136–140
  seeking advice, 72
  sports. *See* Sports and college admissions
  using the Internet, 69–73
  visual arts, 140–142
College visits, 155–159, 192
Common Application, 177, 179–183
Community colleges, 67–68
Community service, 43–44
Complete Book of Colleges, 69
Computers
  buying one's own or using at college, 209–210
  helpful websites. *See* Websites
Cooperative education, 112
Cooperative Entrance Exam (COOP), 39–40
Correspondence courses, 84
Costs, college, 68, 89–91
  books, 91
  paying. *See* Financing college
  room and board, 90–91
  travel, 91
  tuition and fees, 90
  tuition freezing, 110

D
Deafness, 202–203. *See also* Disabilities, students with
Demonstrated Financial Need, 92
Disabilities, students with, 121
  Attention Deficit Disorder (ADD), 80
  Attention Deficit/Hyperactivity Disorder (AD/HD), 204–207
  blindness or visual impairment, 200–201
  checklists, 199–201, 203, 206–207
  college admissions tests, 80, 198, 200
  deafness or hearing impairment, 202–203
  Learning Disabled (LD) students, 204–207
Drinking on campus, 215
Dual enrollment (high school and college), 83

E
EFC (Expected Family Contribution), 91–92
Eighth grade
  class ranking, relative unimportance of, 30–33
  high-school entrance tests, 38–40
    Cooperative Entrance Exam (COOP), 39–40
    High School Placement Test (HSPT), 39
    Independent School Entrance Examination (ISEE), 38–39
    Secondary School Admission Test (SSAT), 39
  ninth grade, what to expect in, 34–38
  planning high school classes, 26–29
  setting goals, 20–25
  starting college planning, 17–19
  student profile, 27
Eleventh grade
  choosing a college, 123–132
    checklists, 127–132, 134–135
    college visits, 155–159
    getting organized, 159–162
    highly selective schools, 127

(*continued*)
Honors Programs, 132–135
painting, drawing, and sculpting, 140–142
performing arts, 136–140
sports. *See* Sports and college admissions
college admission tests, 119–122
getting things done before senior year, 119
students with disabilities, 121
Engineering colleges, 68
Essay, application, 172–174
Internet sites that provide assistance in writing, 174
steps in writing, 174
Expected Family Contribution (EFC), 91–92
Extracurricular activities, 4, 43–44, 50–51

F
FAFSA (Free Application for Federal Student Aid), 91, 93–100, 116, 218
Family Financial Profile (FFP), 100–101
Federal Direct Student Loan Program, 105–106
Federal merit scholarship grants, 103
Federal Parent Loans for Undergraduate Students (PLUS), 105, 107
Federal Pell Grants, 107–108
Federal Supplemental Educational Opportunity Grant Program (SEOG), 108
Federal Work-Study (FWS) Program, 106, 108
Female athletes, 152
Female-only college environment, 69
FFP (Family Financial Profile), 100–101
Financial Aid Profile, 100–101
Financing college, 19
costs, 68, 89–91
books, 91
room and board, 90–91

(*continued*)
travel, 91
tuition and fees, 90
Demonstrated Financial Need, 92
Expected Family Contribution (EFC), 91–92
Financial Aid Profile, 100–101
Free Application for Federal Student Aid (FAFSA), 91, 93–100, 116, 218
getting college credit in high school, 104
grants, 107–108
loans. *See* Loans
lowering costs, 111–112
AmeriCorps, 112
cooperative education, 112
loan forgiveness programs, 111
spending tips, 112
two-year colleges, 111–112
monthly payment plans, 110
outside sources, 109
saving, 87–89
scholarships. *See* Scholarships
tax programs, 109
timetable, eighth through twelfth grades, 115–116
tuition freezing, 110
websites for financial aid, 113–114
Free Application for Federal Student Aid (FAFSA), 91, 93–100, 116, 218
FWS (Federal Work-Study) Program, 106, 108

G
Gifted students, 207–208
Goals, setting, 20–25
Grade point average (GPA), 30, 32–33
Grades, importance of, 1–2
Grants, 107–108

H
Hearing impairment, 202–203. *See also* Disabilities, students with

High school
entrance tests, 38–40
getting college credit in, 104
planning classes in eighth grade, 26–29
support (or lack of support) in college search, 3
9th grade. *See* Ninth grade
10th grade. *See* Tenth grade
11th grade. *See* Eleventh grade
12th grade. *See* Twelfth grade
High School Placement Test (HSPT), 39
Home schooling, 35–36
Home School Legal Defense Association, 36
Honors Programs, 132–135
Hope Scholarship Credit, 109
Housing deposits, 192
HSPT (High School Placement Test), 39

I
IB (International Baccalaureate) program, 81–86, 120, 122
Independent scholarships, 102–103
Independent School Entrance Examination (ISEE), 38–39
Independent study, 84
International Baccalaureate (IB) program, 81–86, 120, 122
Internet. *See* Websites
ISEE (Independent School Entrance Examination), 38–39
Ivy League schools, 127

J
Joint cooperative course programs (high school and college), 83
Junior colleges, 150–151

L
Latin, benefits of studying, 27–28
Learning Disabled (LD) students, 80, 204–207. *See also* Disabilities, students with
Learning style, 5–6
Life Time Learning Tax Credit, 109
Loan forgiveness programs, 111
Loans, 104–107
parents, 107
subsidized, 106
unsubsidized, 106–107

M
Medical schools, 126
Merit scholarships, 102–103
Middle school. *See* Eighth grade
Military academies, 51–58, 65–66
military preparatory school, 53
military websites, 65–66
regular ROTC program, 65
ROTC scholarships, 65
Monthly payment plans, 110

N
National Association of Intercollegiate Athletics (NAIA), 151
National Collegiate Athletic Association (NCAA), 145–150
National Merit Scholarship Program, 102, 120
National Small College Athletic Association (NSCAA), 151
Ninth grade
extracurricular activities, 50–51
military academies, 51–58, 65–66
military preparatory school, 53
military websites, 65–66
regular ROTC program, 65
ROTC scholarships, 65
resume, preparing, 43–49
samples, 45–48, 54–64
NSCAA (National Small College Athletic Association), 151

P
Packing list, 213–214

Parents
life after student has left for college, 216–218
loans from, 107
support (or lack of support) in college search, 3
Parochial schools, 34, 36
Paying for college. *See* Financing college
Payment plans, 110
Pell Grants, 107–108
Performing arts, 49, 136–140
auditions, 136–139
Perkins Loans, 106
Peterson's College & University Almanac, 69
PLAN (Preliminary ACT), 76, 122
PLUS (Parent Loans for Undergraduate Students) loans, 105, 107
Preparatory school, 53, 150
Private colleges, costs of, 68
Private school, 34
PSAT (Preliminary Scholastic Assessment Test), 76–80, 102, 119–120, 122
Public colleges, costs of, 68
Public school, 34
Public speaking skills, 15

R
Reading
authors recommended by colleges, list of, 11–12
as a habit, 8–12
importance for college admissions tests, 9
Recommendations, teacher, 165–166
Religious-affiliated colleges, 68
Resume, preparing, 43–49
samples, 45–48, 54–64
Risks, taking, 7–8
Rolling admissions, 192–193

S
Safety at college, 214–215
SAR (Student Aid Report), 94
SAT (Scholastic Assessment Test), 9, 19, 28, 76, 102, 119–122, 146, 167
Scams
credit cards, 211
ID cards, 211
scholarships, 73, 103, 114
Scholarships, 101–104
federal merit scholarship grants, 103
independent scholarships, 102–103
ROTC scholarships, 65
scams, 73, 103, 114
scholarship search companies, 103
White House Presidential Scholars, 169
Scholastic Assessment Test (SAT), 9, 19, 28, 76, 102, 119–122, 146, 167
Secondary School Admission Test (SSAT), 39
Selective colleges, 127
SEOG (Supplemental Educational Opportunity Grant) Program, 108
Single-sex colleges, 69
Speed-reading, 10
Sports and college admissions, 142–154
checklist, 153–154
female athletes, 152
National Collegiate Athletic Association (NCAA), 145–150
academic eligibility requirements, 147–149
letter of intent, 150
options outside the NCAA, 150–152
junior colleges, 150–151
National Association of Intercollegiate Athletics (NAIA), 151
National Small College Athletic Association (NSCAA), 151
prep schools, 150
websites, 152
SSAT (Secondary School Admission Test), 39
Stafford loans, 105–106

Student Aid Report (SAR), 94
Study environment, 6
Study groups, 7
Studying skills, 1–7
Subsidized loans, 106
Summer before college
  budgeting, 210–212
  moving day, 216
  packing list, 213–214
  parents' life after student has moved, 216–218
  safety concerns, 214–215
  your own computer, 209–210
Summer experiences, 33–34
Supplemental Educational Opportunity Grant (SEOG) Program, 108
Survival
  getting organized, 2
  good grades, 1–2
  parents, school, and you, 3
  public speaking skills, 15
  reading as a habit, 8–12
  student profile, 12–13
  studying, 1–7
  taking risks, 7–8
  time management skills, 3–7
  writing skills, 13–14
    what colleges want in your writing, 14

T
Talented students, 207–208
Tax programs, 109
Teacher recommendations, 165–166
Tenth grade
  Advanced Placement (AP) program, 81–86
  International Baccalaureate (IB) program, 81–86
  PSAT and other tests, 76–80
  selecting a college, 67–75
    admissions staff, 72
    comparison list, 73–75
(*continued*)
    seeking advice, 72
    using the Internet, 69–73
Test of English as a Foreign Language (TOEFL), 76–77, 122
Test of Written English (TWE), 122, 167
Tests, college admissions. *See* College admissions tests
Thank-you notes, 194
Time management skills, 3–7
TOEFL (Test of English as a Foreign Language), 76–77, 122
Tuition, 90. *See also* Costs, college
  freezing, 110
TWE (Test of Written English), 122, 167
Twelfth grade
  college acceptance, 192–193
  college admissions tests, 167–168
  college applications, 172–174
  interview with admissions officers, 170–172
  staying organized, 184–192
  teacher recommendations, 165–166
  thank-you notes, 194
  timeline
    October through December, 168–170
    September, 166–168
Two-year colleges, 111–112

U
United States Air Force Academy, 51
United States Coast Guard Academy, 51–52
United States Merchant Marine Academy, 51
United States Military Academy, 51
United States Naval Academy, 51
Universities, difference from colleges, 67
Unsubsidized loans, 106–107

V
Visiting colleges, 155–159, 192

Visual arts, 49, 140–142
Visual impairment, 200–201. *See also* Disabilities, students with
Vocabulary, building by reading, 9
Volunteer experience, 33–34

W

Websites
  Advanced Placement (AP) program, 83
  career interests, 25
  college admissions test information, 79–80
  college application essay writing assistance, 174
  college applications online, 178–179
  college newspapers, 158
  college selection, 69–73

(*continued*)
  financial aid, 113–114
  Free Application for Federal Student Aid (U.S. Department of Education), 91
  home schooling information, 36
  International Baccalaureate (IB) program, 83
  scholarship scams, 73, 114
  sports and college admissions, 152
  U.S. military, 65–66
Work experience, 43–44, 50–51
Work-Study Program, 106
World Wide Web. *See* Websites
Writing skills, 13–14
  application essay, 172–174
  what colleges want in your writing, 14

About the Author

Jill F. VonGruben, M.A.

Jill F. VonGruben, M.A., is the author of *College Countdown: The Parent's and Student's Survival Kit for the College Admissions Process* which is based upon a self-published book (*Taming the Paper Monster: The College Game*) used by principals, guidance counselors, and schools throughout the nation.

Jill has spent 20 years in an advocacy role in gifted education. For the last eight years, she has specialized in the area of high school academics. She served on the Board of the St. Louis Association of Gifted Education, the founding Board of the Parent Advocates for Gifted Education (as middle school and high school liaisons), and was instrumental in founding the PTO for Rockwood School District's Center for Creative Learning.

Jill is the parent of two college students. The College Countdown was realized not only from her family's experiences, but from interviews with hundreds of parents and college admissions representatives.

Tear Out Card 1

Kaplan
888 Seventh Avenue
New York, NY 10106
(800) 527-8378
http://www.kaplan.com

FastWEB
Financial Aid Search Through the WEB
http://www.fastweb.com

ACT (American College Testing)
2201 North Dodge Street
P.O. Box 168
Iowa City, IA 52243-0168
(319) 337-1000
FAX (319) 339-3021
http://www.act.org

AP (Advanced Placement Exam) Services
P.O. Box 6671
Princeton, NJ 08541-6671
(609) 771-7300
(888) CALL-4-AP
http://collegeboard.org/ap/

CASHE
(major independent scholarship search online)
http://www.cashe.com

International Baccalaureate (IB)
North America & Carribbean
200 Madison Avenue
Suite 2301
New York, NY 10016
(212) 696-4464
FAX (212) 889-9242
http://www.ibo.org

PSAT, SAT I, SATI I, TOEFL, CLEP exams
College Board
P.O. Box 6720
Princeton, NJ 08541-6720
(609) 771-7070
FAX (609) 530-0482
TTD (609) 882-4118
http://www.collegeboard.org

US Department of Education
400 Maryland Avenue, SW
Washington, DC 20202
(800) USA-LEARN
TDD (800) 437-0833
FAX (202) 401-0689

General Information
http://www.ed.gov

FAFSA
(U.S. Department of Education)
(800) 433-3243
TDD (800) 730-8913
http://www.fafsa.ed.gov

Educational Testing Service (ETS)
(Administers AP, SAT I, SAT II exams)
Rosedale Road
Princeton, NJ 08541
(609) 921-9000
http://www.ets.org

Tear Out Card 2A

TESTING TIME LINE

Freshman	ACT and/or SAT I for practice, if warranted
Sophomore	
Fall	PSAT (Preliminary SAT) in October for practice, if warranted PLAN (Preliminary ACT) SAT I ACT
Spring	SAT II (subject area tests), if warranted AP (Advanced Placement) subject area tests, if warranted
Junior	
Fall	PSAT-actual, in October, if warranted Only way into National Merit Scholarship programs SAT I ACT TOEFL, if appropriate
Spring	SAT II (subject area tests), if warranted AP (Advanced Placement) subject area tests, if warranted IB (International Baccalaureate) subject area tests, if warranted
Senior	
Fall	SAT I, if needed ACT, if needed TOEFL, if appropriate and needed SAT II (subject area tests), if needed for admission TWE (Test of Written English)
Spring	AP (Advanced Placement) subject area tests IB (International Baccalaureate) subject area tests

Tear Out Card 2B

Make a master schedule of dates, schools, etc. to be posted in a family open space, for example a kitchen, so that everyone knows and can help keep track of when the deadlines are so none are missing. It also helps knowing when the high stress times will hit.

SAMPLE MASTER COLLEGE COUNTDOWN SCHEDULE

Senior Year

May

5/1 Pull together all of the offers and make a final decision.

April

Start pulling together the offers as they come in.

March

3/15 Independent scholarship applications due.

February

2/15-2/20 Make sure SAR is correct and reported back to colleges.
2/15 or so receive SAR back

January

FAFSA needs to be filed
1/15 College applications due

December

Winter Break: fill out applications due in January
12/1 College applications due

November

11/15 College applications due

October

10/15 Independent scholarship application due
10/1 College application due

September

2nd week National Merit announces Semi-Finalists
Attend Open Houses
Take SAT/ACT again
Find out school's procedure for handling applications, scholarships, etc.

Tear Out Card 3

FINANCIAL AID TIMELINE FOR 12TH GRADE

12th Grade

- Apply to colleges and file any Profiles and individual college specific financial aid forms, as required.
- In November and December, obtain FAFSA form from high school guidance counseling office/counselor.
- Attend free college financial aid workshops.
- December, fill out the FAFSA as completely as possible.
- January, file FAFSA using estimated tax document figures.
- February, receive the Student Aid Report (SAR) which is the results of the FAFSA.
- As soon as possible, complete your Federal 1040 tax return and then re-file your updated SAR reflecting the actual figures used in your tax return.
- February-March, receive corrected SAR based on atual tax return data.
- March-April, receive college financial aid notification (award letters) from all colleges to which you have been accepted.
- Compare all awards and proceed with any negotiations, if necessary.
- May 1st, finalize your decision and notify the colleges of that decision.
- May-July, Apply for any loans needed.

(Note: Please refer to chapters 3-5 for more detailed information regarding the financial aid process and financial preparation.)

Tear Out Card 4A

SAMPLE QUESTIONS TO ASK DURING THE ADMISSIONS INTERVIEW

What is the availability of undergraduate research?

How long has the department for my major been in existence?

What are the safety support programs on campus?

How many freshman courses are taught by:

Professors?

Grad students?

What is an example of some of the extracurricular activities and clubs on campus?

What are the university's study abroad programs and what percentage of the student body participates?

I am really active in ____________________ in high school, how can I expand that leadership role at your school?

Do your performing arts groups (choirs, orchestras, plays, musicals) allow participation by non-majors?

Do you have intramural or club sports?

I have this particular disability, how can I work in partnership with your staff to be successful here?

What are the community service opportunities at your campus?

Tear Out Card 4B

SAMPLE OF THINGS TO ASK A COLLEGE

What's the total enrollment of the college?

What is the size of the freshman class?

What is the enrollment in your desired program?

What are the computer and network capabilities of the campus and how are the dorm rooms wired?

What are the dorm rooms like and what are the residency requirements for freshmen?

What are the regulations for freshman having cars on campus?

How is campus-life on campus?

What are your safety concerns?

How close are you to shops and stores?

Tear Out Card 4C

SAMPLE QUESTIONS TO CONSIDER ABOUT YOURSELF WHEN PICKING A COLLEGE

Do I want to go to school close to home? Would I rather just go home a few times a year?

Do I want to be in a small, individualized environment? Is being a number amongst thousands okay?

Do I have any medical or physical issues that will require extra attention in college?

Can I share a room with 1, 2, or even 3 roommates?

Would I feel comfortable in a co-ed dorm or floor?

Do I have a major in mind yet?

How will I pay for college?

How are my high school grades and test scores?

How hard do I want to work in college?

Do I want to join a Frat or Sorority?

Tear Out Card 5

STUDENT RESUMÉ WORKSHEET

University Name ______________________________

Application for Admission to the Class of ______________________________

Student Name ______________________________

Social Security Number ______________________________

LIST ANY EMPLOYMENT, VOLUNTEER WORK, OR SUMMER STUDY EXPERIENCE

Grade(s)	Activity	Hours per wk

EXTRACURRICULAR ACTIVITIES

A. School

Grade(s)	Activity	Hours per wk

B. Interscholastic Athletics

Grade(s)	Activity	Hours per wk

C. Community Service

Grade(s)	Activity	Hours per wk

AWARDS

Grade(s)	Activity

Tear Out Card 6A

THE GROCERY LIST OF WHAT TO GIVE YOUR GUIDANCE COUNSELOR WHEN SUBMITTING YOUR APPLICATION

The high school application cover form with:

- What college and mailing address
- A list of what needs to be included
- Deadlines
- Your signature and date
- Application, dated and signed
- Fee, check or money order
- Recommendations
- Resumé, if on separate sheet
- Transcript

Tear Out Card 6B

For everyone who helped you along the way, wrote recommendations, processed paper and encouraged you, remember to say or write your "thank yous."

SAMPLE OF THANK YOU FOR RECOMMENDATIONS

Date

Mrs.______________

High School

Dear Mrs.______________

Thank you very much for writing the recommendations for me for my college admissions applications. They really helped.

Sincerely,

____